JABEZ

JABEZ

The Rise and Fall of a Victorian Rogue

•

David McKie

•

Atlantic Books
London

First published in Great Britain
in 2004 by Atlantic Books,
an imprint of Grove Atlantic Ltd

1 2 3 4 5 6 7 8 9

A CIP catalogue record for this book is available
from the British Library.

ISBN 1 84354 130 0

Printed in Great Britain by CPD, Ebbw Vale, Wales.

Atlantic Books
An imprint of Grove Atlantic Ltd
Ormond House
26–27 Boswell Street
London WC1N 3JZ

And Jabez was more honourable than his brethren:
and his mother called his name Jabez, saying,
Because I bare him with sorrow.

And Jabez called on the God of Israel, saying, Oh that thou
wouldest bless me indeed, and enlarge my coast, and that
thine hand might be with me, and that thou wouldest keep
me from evil, that it may not grieve me! And God granted
him that which he requested.

I Chronicles 4: 9–10

It was beautiful and simple, as all the great swindles are.

O. Henry, The Octopus Marooned

Contents

Illustrations

Text Illustrations

Plates

The author and publishers are grateful to the following for permission to reproduce images: Part One, National Portrait Gallery, London; Part Two, 2, 3, 4, 5, Croydon Local Studies Library; 1, Janet Cunliffe-Jones; 6, 9, 10, 11, 12, Hulton Archive / Getty Images; 7, Royal Geographical Society; 14, British Library.

Preface

Edward Smith was a warder in Portland jail in the 1890s. He was also my wife's grandfather. In the summer of 1996, we went to Portland, that eerie, unsettling island community just off the coast of Dorset, in the hope of getting a sense of the place where he had lived and the prison he had worked in. That prison is a young offenders' institution now, and you do not see much of it from the street. But we found in the library across the water in Weymouth some descriptions of Portland prison as it would have been when Smith worked there. One of these was an evocation of the prison in the late 1890s as 'a heart-breaking, soul-enslaving, brain-destroying hell upon earth'. The man who had written these words, it added, was a former Liberal MP sentenced to fourteen years imprisonment for his part in a massive fraud.

This was odd. For though I had a working knowledge of Members of Parliament jailed for wrong-doing, from Horatio Bottomley through to John Stonehouse, and others, like Robert Maxwell, who deserved the same fate but escaped it, the name in this case was a new one: Jabez Spencer Balfour. Why had I never heard of him? I looked up his obituary and the news reports of his death in *The Times* and began taking notes: the creation and the prospering of his business empire, based on his Liberator Building Society, the huge crash of 1892, the unravelling of the fictitious transactions on which his apparent success had been built, his escape to Argentina after some of his closest associates were arrested, and his fight by all kinds of ingenious means to stay there, his nemesis at the hands of a detective sent out by Scotland Yard, the epic journey which took him back to London and justice, his trial and sentence, his death on a railway train on his way, at seventy-two, to start a new job: all these made his story still more intriguing.

In a box in Burnley Library – Jabez had been the town's MP before his disgrace – I found an account of him by David Rock, who had grown up in Burnley and who, as Professor of Latin American history at the University of California, Santa Barbara, had researched the fugitive's time in Argentina and written an exhilarating record of it. In the local studies library at Croydon, where Jabez was mayor, I found a devastating analysis of his fraud published after the crash by the *Westminster Gazette*, and the eccentric account by an Argentinian journalist of his journey upcountry to Salta to interview Jabez, which I've drawn on in chapter 9 of this book.

And trawling through an electronic newspaper archive I discovered pieces about Jabez Balfour by Richard Lambert of the *Financial Times* (who later became its editor), who plainly found him as fascinating as I did. By a wonderful piece of good fortune, one of these had caught the eye of Mrs Janet Cunliffe-Jones, great-granddaughter of Jabez's brother John Lucas Balfour, and she had written to the newspaper with some recollections of her black sheep great-great-uncle. Mrs Cunliffe-Jones most generously let me see the papers she had about Jabez, including an account by her father Sir Hugo Marshall of the life of John Lucas Balfour and his quarrel with Jabez, together with her own unfinished biography of Jabez's mother Clara Lucas Balfour, whose achievements as lecturer, writer and feminist heroine make her well worth a book of her own. She has also heroically transcribed notes and letters in the villainous handwriting of John Lucas Balfour. What I know of Jabez's childhood is almost entirely due to Janet.

I had started by thinking the story would make a newspaper article; by this stage I had begun to think it might furnish a book. So did my agent, Mike Shaw, at Curtis Brown, who was hugely enthusiastic from the start. And so too, in time, with the resolute encouragement of my friend and colleague Simon Hoggart, did Toby Mundy at Atlantic Books. Another publisher had decided not to proceed on the grounds that though the story sounded intriguing, when the name Jabez Balfour was raised at their staff conference, no one present had ever heard of him. That was the very reason, of course, why I thought he might be worth writing about. Happily Toby thought that way too.

The late Sheila Llewellyn, then surmounting infirmity to finish a history of Burcot, where Jabez was squire, steered me painstakingly through her material. Her millennium commemoration of Burcot and Clifton Hampden is one of many such books published across the country which will still be read and enjoyed when we've long forgotten the Millennium Dome. Paula Lugones in Buenos Aires and Dr Alfonso Assini and John Hooper in Rome made enquiries about Jabez's mistress on my behalf, though sadly the records for which they were searching could not be found. The London Library, the City of London's library at Guildhall, the National Archive and the British Library, and especially its Colindale newspaper satellite, have all been essential. But I also want to thank librarians and archivists at Croydon, Burnley, Tamworth, Weymouth, Newport Isle of Wight, Doncaster, Bedfordshire and Luton, the London boroughs of Southwark and Brent, and Surrey County Cricket Cricket Club all of whom have been helpful and some of whom have pointed me in directions I might otherwise not have thought about.

Simon Hoggart and Judy Goodman read the draft of the book, made many helpful suggestions, and picked up some of my errors. Jane Robertson expertly honed my original text and Clara Farmer and Bonnie Chiang at Atlantic Books shepherded it through with warm support and patient attention. My final debt is to my wife Beryl, not only for providing me with my link to Edward Smith, and so to Portland and Jabez, but for her enthusiasm and support for this project; and for compiling the index. This book is dedicated to her.

The texts at the head of the chapters are taken from the *Congregational Hymnary* as Jabez would have known it at the end of his life.

•

Part One

•

I

Young Jabez

Keep thou our boyhood free and fair,
And quick to help and brave to dare,
From greed and selfishness and shame
Guard thou, O Lord, the English name

John Macleod Campbell Crum (1872–1958)

On a bitter morning in February 1916, a travelling railway official called Percy Henry Keen entered a third-class smoking carriage on the London to Fishguard express and asked to see the tickets of the three men he found there. Two quickly complied, but the third did not stir. He seemed to be deeply asleep. Keen touched him gently, first on the knee, then on the arms and the shoulder. Still no response. 'He appears to have gone off very sound,' said the ticket collector. He'd been quite all right a moment ago, the other passengers told him, and had been chattering away cheerfully about his recent experiences in Burma. 'He looks ill,' Keen said, and went to summon the guard. The train was searched for a doctor, but none could be found. As it passed Severn tunnel junction, the guard threw out a message, asking that a doctor be summoned to Newport station. But well before Newport it was clear that

3

the man was dead. The cause, the Newport coroner later concluded, was heart failure.

But who was the dead man? His pockets were searched. There was money to the value of £1 19s 4d, stamps, a pipe, a metal watch, and a railway ticket for Landore, just outside Swansea, and some letters, which gave them his name: Jabez Spencer Balfour. 'The Jabez Spencer Balfour,' as the Newport coroner was later to say to his court, 'of Liberator notoriety.' This was a man once condemned in England as 'the greatest thief of the nineteenth century', 'a criminal of colossal dimensions'; and described by *The Times*, as 'a man of cold-blooded villainy… one of the most impudent and heartless scoundrels on record'.

His notoriety had grown to be international. The *New York Times* wrote of him when he was brought back to face trial: 'The return of Jabez Spencer Balfour from Argentina… is a triumph of law. Prud'hon's painting of *Justice Pursuing Crime* is not more impressive.' It called him 'a learned hypocrite' and talked of 'a well-laid plan of piety by which he gained confidence, popularity, and situation, and ruined the poor'. Though the man was 'a thick, gorged, bloated monstrosity, rotund, wallowsome and flat footed', people in England, the *Sydney Bulletin* said, had believed in him with a profound and childlike faith. 'He was obtrusively and aggressively pious,' it wrote, 'and though his coarse and pimpled visage was a visible warning to everyone who saw him, the Anglo-Saxon's trust in broadcloth and snuffle enabled him to overcome these disadvantages.'

But the deepest resentment, the most bitter condemnation,

came from those whose lives he had wrecked. Some, contemplating the life of destitution which awaited them after his companies had crashed, killed themselves; others went mad. Such was the popular hatred after he fled to Argentina and resisted all attempts to return him, that his effigy was burned on Bonfire Night. 'You will never be able,' said the judge who eventually sentenced him, 'to shut from your ears the cries of the widows and orphans you have ruined.'

Jabez Balfour was born on 4 September 1843, the son of what must have seemed an oddly assorted marriage. His mother, Clara Lucas Balfour, was a person of consequence: an author, a famous temperance campaigner and, in an age when such things were thought unseemly, a lecturer on literature and the status of women. Her book *Morning Dewdrops, or, The Juvenile Abstainer*, first published in the year of Jabez's birth, with its uplifting account of how ancient Britons, given to heavy drinking, were conquered by the more abstemious Romans, was a staple of the temperance cause for seventy years. Her volumes of verse, especially *The Garland of Water Flowers*, were hailed by fellow campaigners as 'exquisite'. Her pamphlet on marriage guidance, *A Whisper to the Newly Married*, published in 1850, went through twenty-three editions. But Clara Balfour could also write sterner stuff: her pamphlet opposing the socialist notions of Robert Owen (mainly, it seemed, because she thought his views on marriage would promote promiscuity) so impressed Jane Welsh Carlyle, wife of the historian Thomas Carlyle, that she sought Clara out and made a friend of her.

Clara's level-headed resolution reflected an early life of harsh circumstance. 'Should the readers of these pages be seeking a healthy stimulation to overcome all obstacles,' her daughter Cecil would later write in a memoir of her, 'they may gather encouragement from the story of one whose days of girl-hood were days of sorrow and hard discipline.' Jabez believed her example had inspired Samuel Smiles.

She was born in 1808, out of wedlock. Her great-great-grand-daughter, Janet Cunliffe-Jones, suspected that Clara's extrovert father John Lyddell Lucas was married already when her mother Sarah took up with him. A butcher and cattle dealer trading in Gosport and on the Isle of Wight, he did not live with Sarah, but for several years took charge of Clara and arranged for her education. But he died when Clara was nine, leaving her wholly dependent on Sarah, who, at just twenty-nine, was stern, sad and resentful. Money was short, and Sarah moved to London, where she and Clara struggled to make a living by needlework. Only her love of books redeemed Clara's dull life. Her formal education was fitful. Now and then there was money enough to send her to a boarding school at Woodford in Essex, but when times were bad her mother recalled her. She had no regular schooling after the age of thirteen.

And then in 1824 – at nearly sixteen – she married James Balfour, or 'little Jimmy Balfour' as he was known. He was twelve years older than she was, and had joined the navy as a ship's boy – more a servant to officers than a real sailor – surviving a shipwreck before deserting. His subsequent boasts when among his family of having seen service at Trafalgar were not taken seriously, presumably even by him, since he would have been only eight at the time.

The early years of Clara's marriage can hardly have been more comfortable than the difficult life with her mother. James ran what some records call a marine store, though other accounts call it a rag and bone and bottle shop, in Chelsea. He is also said to have been at various times a mattress-maker, street trader and locksmith. By the time of Jabez's birth, however, Jimmy had risen in the world. The boy's birth certificate lists him as 'temperance lecturer', though unlike Clara he was valued less for sweet-tongued persuasiveness than for his readiness to preach the doctrines of temperance in the rougher parts of London. He did so with a courage born perhaps of experience: for where Clara took the pledge out of principle, Jimmy seems to have done so in a bid to break what one of the Balfours' friends described as 'habits of inebriation'. Despite attempts to redeem himself when returning home drunk by bringing a prayer book as a present for Clara, his addiction put the household under great strain. Her daughter Cecil's account of her mother's early married life speaks of 'tribulation' and 'untold sorrow'. 'There only came a dawning of brighter times,' she says 'when the habits were changed of the one who had promised to protect and support her.'

Jimmy also found work at the Palace of Westminster. The 1861 census lists him as 'messenger, House of Commons'; ten years later, 'messenger' has been upgraded to 'official'. He worked mainly in the Ways and Means corridor of the Commons, probably as an assistant to more senior officials. By this time, too, he had expanding business interests: he was one of the founders, in 1856, of the Temperance Building Society, of which he became a director. In the letters that Clara wrote to her children, their father comes across as a fondly regarded but rather preoccupied and occasionally irritable presence.

The Balfours had seven children. The first, a boy, was born dead the day after Clara's seventeenth birthday. The second, Arthur, born in 1827, died at nineteen, in August 1847, 'poisoned by corrosive sublimate' according to his death certificate. He took the poison in a public park close to his home near Paddington Green, and the illness which drove him to it was clearly very severe. Clara, at any rate, was relieved that his sufferings were over: 'It is better that he should be in his grave than in a madhouse ... I am thankful that my poor boy has escaped the miseries of a madhouse, and reached a world where there is no cloud to dim the intellect.'

Cecil, their only daughter, was born in 1829; and John Lucas – named after his Gosport grandfather – two years later. Another two years and a fifth child was born, a boy who lived just a few days. Two years more, and a further son arrived, James Lucas. Finally, after an interval of more than eight years, during which time Clara's career had prospered, and she had reached the age of thirty-five, which in those days was late for childbirth, there was born on September 1843, a son whom they christened Jabez Spencer Balfour.

Jabez was a good biblical name, then still modestly popular in Victorian England. It is usually translated as meaning 'born in sorrow', though it can also mean 'he will cause pain and sorrow', as indeed this one would. According to one account, Jabez Balfour 'wrought more woe and misery in English households than anything that has happened since the South Sea Bubble'. The story of Jabez, much savoured in non-conformist homes of the kind he was later to blight, is told in the first book of Chronicles, chapter 4, verses 9 and 10.

This Jabez was named after his godfather, the Revd Dr Jabez Burns, a prominent Baptist minister and crusader for temperance, three years older than Clara and nine younger than James. The power of his preaching had brought Clara under his spell, and when the household moved from Chelsea to Paddington, their new address was close to the chapel in Church Street, off Edgware Road, where Burns was minister. His son Dawson, also a Baptist minister and champion of temperance, would in time marry Jabez's sister Cecil. As for Jabez's middle name, Spencer, this too seems to have had a temperance connection. Like Dr Burns, the Revd Thomas Spencer was a non-conformist minister prayerfully energetic in the temperance cause.

Jabez's brothers and sister had been born when the household was poor and his surviving brothers had only a perfunctory schooling before being sent out to make their way in the world. By the time Jabez was born, the Burns family's fortunes had changed very much for the better. By now, Clara's reputation was bringing crowds to the lecture halls: in one venue, where they both appeared within weeks of each other, she drew as big an attendance as the American poet and essayist, Ralph Waldo Emerson. The fees she commanded, though often less than were paid to her male counterparts, were handsome by Balfour standards. She was much in demand, in Ireland as well as in England and Wales, for the beauty of her delivery as much as her content. Sometimes she took Jabez with her on tour. Her youngest and last, he seemed a particular favourite, his doings and sayings described in fond detail when she wrote to his brothers. He made friends easily, she reported to her son John after one such excursion in 1854, 'and talks a great deal' – discussing, aged ten, matters of war and politics with pensioners on park benches. He was clearly exceptionally bright.

And yet there was something along with this cleverness that made her uneasy. 'You ask about Jabez's intellect,' she had written to John soon after the boy was five. 'He is improving greatly. He is as noisy as ever, that is his nature, but I never saw a child with a better memory or quicker intellect. James is a sensible boy, but he has not the mental power that Jabez has. I hope sincerely that dear Jabez will early be brought under right religious influences and then I have no doubt if he is spared he will make a very useful and perhaps a great man.' Then she added – as it turned out, prophetically: 'But I certainly think there is very much to fear as well as hope in his case. He will be either good or evil – there is nothing negative about him.'

If his intellect set him apart from his siblings, so did the way he was schooled. He was sent to school first in France – at Guînes, near Calais, the scene of the Field of the Cloth of Gold – and then to Germany. His mother visited him there, long enough on one of these occasions to write a book called *The Burnish Family*. In his memoir *My Prison Life*, the nearest thing he wrote to an autobiography, Jabez recalled his success at his school in Guînes. 'I remember, with not a little pride,' he wrote, 'that in France I took the first French prize from the French boys after a very keen "international competition".' He prided himself on remaining fluent in French: 'I used as a boy to be fond of riding on the roofs of Parisian omnibuses, and thus became somewhat familiar with Parisian slang.' But foul language, of which he was doomed to hear a great deal when his life turned sour, upset him throughout his days.

His onward and upward path did not extend, as it might have done later, from school to university. Instead, no doubt through his father's influence, he found a job with a firm of parliamentary agents at Westminster. This was in 1860, the year of his seventeenth birthday. He was still describing himself as 'parliamentary agent' at twenty-eight, in the census of 1871, though by then his thoughts had turned to more rewarding opportunities.

James and Clara Balfour had moved out of London by the time he started work, and were living in middle-class comfort in the burgeoning town of Reigate, Surrey. It was there in September 1864 that Jabez celebrated his twenty-first birthday. The Revd Dr Jabez Burns had composed a poem for the occasion – hardly up to the standards of his namesake Robert Burns, but kindly intentioned, and revealing too how close the two families must have been:

I saw thee daily on thy course.
I watched with interest, too
And often wondered what the Boy
Would finally come to...

I saw thee enter on the course
Of thy industrial life.
Then, by the by, whispers I heard
About a little wife...

The whispers were right. On 2 June 1866, Jabez, aged twenty-two, and Ellen Mead, daughter of James Whittle Mead, gentleman, of Westbourne Park Road, London W, who was twenty, were married by Dr Burns at Reigate. They went to live at a good address: White Post Hill, between Reigate and what is now the separate town of Redhill. His little wife beside him, and his hopes of 'enlarging his coast', as the biblical story of Jabez put it, burning brightly, Jabez Balfour was on his way.

2

The Liberator

Happy, who in thy house reside.

John Milton (1608–74)

Ten years on, when the runaway success of his Liberator Building Society was the talk of the City, most people assumed that Jabez Balfour had designed and created it himself. 'The great Liberator', his rivals would mockingly call him. What in fact he had done was to take a scheme which had foundered before and repackage it in a way which promised to catch the eye and bring in the money of a wider audience. Where the failed predecessor had appealed to the growing, but still limited, ranks of the temperance movement, Jabez was out to woo the whole of the non-conformist community of England and Wales. This was a promisingly large constituency, amounting, on the best available estimates, to some 1.6 million people in England and Wales in 1870.

The failed model had been an enterprise called the Alliance National Land, Building and Investment Society, designed to appeal to the temperance movement – its name deliberately echoing that of the principal engine of the British temperance movement, the United Kingdom Alliance, founded in

Manchester in 1853. Dawson Burns, son of the Baptist minister Dr Jabez Burns, had been the sixth member enrolled.

Temperance had a wider appeal than strict teetotalism. Though many temperance people, like Jabez's parents, had signed the pledge and would never let liquor pass their lips, others thought drinking in moderation was acceptable in the right place: in the home, the hotel even – but not in those ungodly haunts of the working class, public houses. Some, like Clara Balfour, resisted this distinction, which for them came too close to demanding one law for the rich and one for the poor.

When Jabez Burns began to preach at Church Street, Edgware Road, in the 1830s, there were said to be only a handful of pulpits in England faithful to the temperance cause. Now there were hundreds. The movement was on the march. In 1862, the Alliance Building Society installed itself in premises over the office of the *Alliance News*, the *Temperance Star* and other organs of the war against drink and published its first prospectus. Dawson Burns was listed simply as auditor, but he and his faithful lieutenant, George Dibley, were more closely involved than that might suggest. The Society was the core of what became the Horner Group of companies, taking its name from its secretary, J. A. Horner. Under the chairmanship of the mellifluously named Harper Twelvetrees, the organization set out not just to lend money to temperance people but to build them good homes to live in. It recruited 300 agents, mostly from the ranks of temperance workers. In 1864, the *Temperance Star* announced the purchase of land in Oxford on which the Horner Group intended to build a temperance colony, from which pubs would be banished for ever.

Soon nine companies had been founded, gathered together under the Estates Bank which suggested a rather wider market than temperance. Some in the temperance movement regretted this change. Mammon, they feared, was becoming more influential than God. But, like the proposed Oxford colony, the whole enterprise was doomed. Founded on high moral principles, but ill equipped for the harsh commercial world into which it had ventured, the Estates Bank failed to survive the turmoil which in 1866 overtook the City of London and brought down a host of companies. The whole Horner Group collapsed, ruining, and in some cases driving to suicide, shareholders and investors. The United Kingdom Alliance, which until now had never denied its connection with the building society, now became eager to do so, requiring that those involved in the Horner Group be removed from its ruling executive.

It was out of the wreckage of this adventure that the Liberator Building Society emerged. The Alliance project might have ended in tears, but the principle on which it was founded – philanthropic finance – was too noble, its champions believed, to be lost. They would try again – and succeed this time. Dawson Burns was deeply involved, and brought on board both his father and two of his brothers-in-law, John Lucas Balfour and Jabez. The younger brother's business acumen, his ability to charm and persuade, his imagination and his eye for an opportunity, made him the Liberator's most effective and glamorous asset. He had soon supplanted his brother John as its secretary, and by 1870 he had risen to be managing director. From then on, the world, from City admirers to thousands of grateful families jingling the keys to homes they could feel truly belonged to them, rightly saw the Liberator as Jabez's enterprise.

The first company to be founded – the Lands Allotment Company – was concerned with the buying of land and the building of houses. But to buy what the LAC intended to offer, customers would need to have funds, and in the existing system of things, many potential customers didn't. The enterprise only took shape when the Liberator Building Society opened its doors for business in June 1868. It adopted the slogan: '*Libera sedes, liberum facit*', or 'a free home makes a free man'. Its proudly proclaimed intention was to bring the benefits of home ownership to non-conformist (and predominantly renting) England and Wales. That was why it had chosen its name. Just as the name 'Alliance' in the earlier venture had implied a closer link than in fact existed with the temperance campaigners of the UK Alliance, so the Liberator hinted at an integral connection with the largest, most powerful engine of non-conformist sentiment in the country – the Liberation Society (or, to give it its full grandiloquent title, the Society for the Liberation of Religion from State Patronage and Control).

The Liberation Society was an umbrella under which non-conformists of every persuasion could gather, committed to bring to an end the established status of the Anglican Church, and to sweep away all the financial devices, such as church rates, by which ordinary people, however opposed they might be to its doctrines and practices, were required to sustain it. Great names from the non-conformist movement, installed in largely ceremonial posts, decorated the Liberator Building Society's letterhead. And though Anglicans dealt with it too, everything about it proclaimed its non-conformist allegiance.

Most of its agents were non-conformist ministers, desperate to augment their meagre stipends. The involvement of men like the Burnses, father and son, seemed to guarantee its integrity, to demonstrate irrefutably its basis of true philanthropy and high moral principle. Its deliberations took place in the odour of sanctity: some board meetings opened with prayers. When the Liberator moved to newer and larger premises, God was formally thanked, in a resolution said to have been drafted by Dawson Burns: 'that on the occasion of taking possession this day of our new premises, the directors desire to record their own sense of thankfulness for the prosperity with which, as they believe, God has hitherto blessed their efforts in the establishment of this business.' Amen.

And certainly they had every reason for gratitude. The Liberator prospered mightily. Its growth was a matter for awe. There had never been a success in the building society movement that came near to matching it. After a mere three years its reported assets had grown to £70,000; after seven, to £500,000. By 1879, it had overtaken the Leeds Permanent to become the biggest building society in the land. And where the Horner Group had ailed and collapsed, the Balfour Group was blossoming at a rate which must have confirmed to those who met at its boardroom table that God had answered their prayers. In 1875, the House and Lands Investment Trust was established. In 1882, they launched their own bank, the London and General. Three years later, the Building Securities Company joined the merry throng, along with Hobbs and Co., builders of Croydon, and another company begun by a local builder, George Newman and Co. The Real Estates Company was added in 1886. These companies became known as the Balfour Group of companies – or sometimes as the Budge Row Group, from the address of Jabez's City of London headquarters.

By now this had long ceased to be an organization narrowly targeted at the aspirations of non-conformist England: it had become a force throughout the world of building and property, and was destined to leave its lasting mark on the face of the capital with ambitious projects designed by distinguished architects for the rich and successful.

Jabez, as the prime mover – the Skipper, as his colleagues liked to call him – had assembled a faithful group of lieutenants to push his projects through. The inner core, whose names will recur throughout this story, was drawn from three groups: the men whom the *Financial Times* would one day call 'the Croydon capitalists', the temperance tendency, and the City men.

Jabez had set up house in Croydon at the end of the 1860s, and he liked to have Croydon men about him. Of the 'Croydon capitalists', the most devoted and single-minded of all was George Brock. He came from a Baptist family – his father and brother were ministers, his father a very distinguished one –

and had, in common with most of his colleagues, a hinterland which took in piety, good works and Liberal politics. Born in the same year as Jabez, he offered unstinting loyalty, even when dirty work was required, and a wonderful head for figures. He served on the Croydon health board and was secretary of West Croydon Young Men's Association when Jabez was its president. The great advocate Sir Edward Marshall Hall, who defended him for a nominal sum when retribution caught up with him, came to like and admire him.

Francis Moses Coldwells – 'the little alderman', as he was known in Croydon – was sixteen years older than Jabez, and another unswerving loyalist, whose particular value for Jabez was his rise from humble origins and the way he spoke for ordinary working men. Coldwells had come from Essex to manage a nursery on the fringes of Croydon, though he later became a partner in an outfitting business. Whenever Jabez needed to offer a guarantee that, although an employer and indeed a mine-owner, he kept the interests of working people close to his heart, there was Alderman Coldwells, a presence in all his master's parliamentary campaigns. Coldwells had his own parliamentary ambitions too, winning Lambeth North for the Liberals in 1892. Though some Croydon Conservatives felt the presence of a man of such humble origins was proof of how low the place had now fallen, he was generally well regarded there. His adopted home town recognized him as a man who had helped clear its cluttered streets, build a new town hall, and save its public space on the Addington Hills from enclosure.

James William Hobbs had risen from humble beginnings too. He was born in 1843 – the same year as Jabez and Brock – in Portsmouth: his father, who died when the boy was eleven, was in the construction business but had always wanted to be a musician, and instilled a love of music into his son to a point where he too wanted to make it his life. But his family needed a steady wage and Hobbs became an apprentice joiner. He moved to Croydon, where he was introduced to Jabez Spencer Balfour, 'whose name will always be honoured in Croydon'. He began his own business as a timber and mahogany merchant in Morland Road, north of the town, which developed into a building company and in 1885 became a Balfour company, Hobbs and Co.

Hobbs, much more than Coldwells or Brock, had high social aspirations. In 1884 he bought – or rather, his company bought for him – a house called Norbury Hall for himself, his wife and ten children (all learning musical instruments, he told the *Croydon Review*) and the nearby Norbury Park. The hall became a place for entertaining and the staging of musical evenings. In the park, he created a cricket ground where the Surrey second eleven played (many of Surrey's players worked for him), where in May 1888 the visiting Australians did battle with C. I. Thornton's XI, and where every summer Hobbs's own team took on the Orleans Club. W. G. Grace was always expected, though he did not often turn up, which was just as well for the opposition since when he did appear one summer he made 93 runs and took seven wickets. This was the kind of occasion Hobbs revelled in. Two marquesses and three lesser lords were on the team sheet and 627 runs were made in the day. Another of these games was graced with the even more dazzling participation of Prince Christian, son of the Queen.

The temperance men were Jabez's brother-in-law Dawson Burns, who would pull out six years before the crash, and Burns's close associate, 'his fidus Achates' (Aeneas's companion in Virgil's *Aeneid*)– George Dibley. Of the City men, the most crucial to Jabez's enterprise was the solicitor H. Granville Wright, partner in Wright, Bonner and Thompson. He in a sense was a Croydon capitalist too, and like the others, a diligent non-conformist. But he did not live and breathe Croydon as the rest of them did. Indeed, once he had left his wife and children and taken up with a Mrs Maybury, he was not often seen in the town, preferring to spend his time at his other properties in Grosvenor Mansions, London, Bletchley, and Lismany, near Ballinasloe in County Galway, where he kept a string of horses and a pack of hounds on his rented estate.

Two others stood out in the City contingent. One was Samuel Rowles Pattison, another solicitor, chairman of the Liberator from its inception, with a high reputation for making the kind of flowery speech which brought a glow to the hearts of shareholders – an accomplishment, said his detractors, which came all the more easily to him because he made it his practice never to look too closely at the figures. The other was Morell Theobald, partner in Theobald Brothers and Miall, accountants. The two Theobalds, Morell and William, were both enmeshed in the Balfour Group, and, in a more honorific role, so too was the celebrated non-conformist leader Edward

Miall; but only Morell was close enough to the action to pay, in the end, a heavy price for it.

Several of this group were also involved with other companies, but none on anything like the same scale as Jabez. His power and influence were generously made available in the City. The list of boardrooms that he adorned grew impressively year by year in the annual returns of the Directory of Directors. For a company whose fortunes were waning, bringing Jabez onto the board seemed a prudent step, and one to which the City was sure to react with favour. They might have their doubts about him, but they had to admit that Jabez Balfour knew what he was doing: his record was proof of that. He chaired the company that was bringing tramways to Croydon (as well as being an influential figure in one which ran railways into the town) and chaired the board of another that was doing the same for Northampton. Even the list of his interests in the *Directory*, impressive though it might seem, omitted substantial items, including the mine he owned at Hockley Hall in Warwickshire, and the enterprise which was perhaps closest of all to his heart, showing him at his most adventurous but also his most foolhardy – the reclamation of Brading Harbour on the coast of the Isle of Wight.

Brading must have had a sentimental appeal for him. His mother had spent part of her childhood in this part of the island, and he grew to share her affection for it. Brading Harbour was a tract of marshland, perhaps 750 acres in all, which at high tide disappeared under the sea, and which at low tide was of little practical use to anyone. Ships could sail up it and moor at a quay alongside Brading High Street. Doomed attempts had been made over the centuries to reclaim the marshland for cultivation while creating a smaller harbour nearer the sea.

The most ambitious scheme, and the only one that ever came near to success, was attempted in the reign of James I. Having no use for it, the king gave the land to a groom of the bedchamber, who sold it on for £2,000 to two businessmen: Sir Bevis Thelwall and Hugh Myddelton, the entrepreneur who had carried through the New River project in London. Having spent a further £7,000 reclaiming the land with the help of a team of Dutchmen, they discovered that the tract they had saved was full of a light running sand and therefore of little commercial value. Moreover, their work was inadequate: in a spell of prolonged wet weather, when the water was exceptionally high, a spring tide swept it into oblivion. A further attempt in the final year of seventeenth century foundered, after which no one appeared brave or rash enough to tackle it again.

This was just the kind of challenge Jabez found hard to resist – one where many before him had failed. The sea until now had vanquished all comers; but Jabez would vanquish the sea. In 1874 he promoted a parliamentary bill which became the Brading Harbour Improvement Railways and Works Act. He would drain the marshes and build a causeway across them, dividing the land he aimed to reclaim from the sea and providing a spendid new harbour for Bembridge. He would bring the railway across from St Helen's to end the isolation of

Bembridge, making it as fine and accessible a resort as Sandown or Shanklin. He would greatly improve and extend the oyster beds. He would run spanking new passenger steamers to Portsmouth. And then he would top it off by building a splendid hotel appropriate to the requirements of the quality and gentry.

In 1878 contractors moved in to build an embankment on much the same line as Myddelton's. 'Day and night, for weeks and months at a stretch,' wrote a local historian 'thousands of tons of chalk and rubble and clay from Bembridge Down and Portsdown Hills came pouring into Bembridge by land and sea, and were dumped down on the site of the embankment, which soon began to show above low water.' Local people watched with scepticism, even contempt. They knew it could never work. But in July 1879 the operation was finished. The sea had been conquered. 'After many ominous shakes of the head from people residing in the locality of St Helen's,' the *Isle of Wight Observer* reported, 'there can be no doubt that Mr Seymour [the chief contractor] has successfully completed the task of keeping back the water from the extensive mud flats which for years have furnished such capital spots for the "winkler" and the fowler.' On 2 August, a cricket match was staged on the reclaimed land between Brading, who made 76, and Brading Harbour, bowled out for 18 and then for 28, with W. Stribling taking ten of their wickets and H. Gladdy another seven. Great was the glory of Stribling and Gladdy; greater still was the glory of Seymour; but the greatest triumph was that of Jabez, who despite all the sneers had always known that the project was going to succeed.

Then one Sunday morning in October the tide demolished the embankment as majestically as it had Myddelton's. At the height of the storm, workmen were drowned and a horse and cart were swept away by the sea. 'The breach has since reached some 70 yards in width,' the *Isle of Wight Observer* dolefully told its readers, 'and the sea has covered the whole of the harbour just the same as it did before the embankment was made. Vessels now come up and down the harbour to Brading Quay for chalk as if nothing had happened to check them.'

Together, Jabez Balfour and his friend and business associate Henry Freeman surveyed the disaster. When Jabez asked him to manage the project, Freeman had been reluctant. It meant cutting himself off from his business in London. It also meant leaving the Surrey town of Sutton and abandoning his dominant and respected role in the politics of the town. But Jabez was accomplished at persuasion, and Freeman succumbed. At a grand farewell banquet in his honour, representatives of Sutton presented him with a handsome silver jug, two goblets and a timepiece. But this was not goodbye: as soon as he could, Freeman declared, he would come back to Sutton. He looked forward to growing old there and dying among them.

So Freeman brought his wife and his extensive family to the pretty village of St Helen's, high above Brading Harbour, and began a new life he would never have sought. And the outcome was the ruinous scene that he now surveyed. Even then, in the face of disaster, the two men resolved they would yet succeed where Myddelton failed. Jabez had no intention of taking second place to the ocean. The work would have to be done all over again.

Before long, the sceptical heads were shaking again as repairs began, with a new embankment built on a slightly altered line from the old one. This time, a local paper reported, they were stuffing the gap with chalk and marl instead of mud and sand; an old barge, loaded with chalk, had been sunk across the gap. In spite of this, said the reporter, the 'salts' of the locality were prophesying that the work would never be a permanent success. Efforts so far, it was reported soon afterwards, had been disheartening and unsuccessful; during the work, a valuable steam engine weighing several tons had fallen into the sea and not been recovered. The barge they had stuck in the gap was lost and had to be replaced by another; a workman called Mursell, pushing a truckload of chalk, stumbled, fell into the sea and was drowned. Another who went to his rescue would have been lost had not the contractor Seymour succeeded in saving him.

Even the overflowing optimism that came to be known as Jabez's trademark was stretched to the limit now. But as spring arrived, there were signs that the sea might this time be beaten. In February 1880, the work was completed, though this time without a cricket match. When storms arrived in the following month the new fortifications stood firm. Critics had forecast that even now, Neptune would recapture what he had lost. 'Nothing but an earthquake or a terrible convulsion,' Henry Freeman wrote to the local paper, 'can ever "restore to Neptune" . . . the haven which we have wrested from his wasteful and powerful grip.' The reclaimed land had been analysed and found to be better than anyone had expected. Now even the sceptical locals had to admire. 'Bembridge,' wrote a local historian, 'found all the blessings of modern civilization showered upon it as by a magician's wand'; though Brading, now cut off for good from the sea, declined to join the euphoria.

This triumph, as it seemed at the time, was celebrated in the manner in which Jabez specialized. Everyone must have a good time, over which he himself would preside, and he would have the best time of all. So a very grand party was laid on, with lashings of food, copiously flowing drink, and extravagant speeches. Most of those present had come for the day by boat from Portsmouth, and there might have been even more speeches had they not been in such a hurry to catch the boat back.

How splendid it seemed, his newly completed Royal Spithead Hotel, surrounded on three sides by water, with its gardens, its croquet lawn and its lavish views of the Solent, especially now that the rain on the way down to Portsmouth had given way to bright sunshine. Jabez, who took the chair, proposed the main toast of the day: 'Success to the Brading Harbour undertaking', coupled with that of the new hotel. Through storm and through sunshine, he told the assembled company, through flood and through gale, they who had built it had experienced almost every vicissitude of fortune. He did not know of an undertaking so large and so important as theirs which had been carried to a successful conclusion in the face of so many discouragements. Their fortunes had changed and their difficulties had vanished when his colleague Mr Freeman had come to their aid – as he had done at a very real sacrifice. Mr Freeman was duly toasted, to which he replied that he could not have done the little he had, had he not been blessed with such an excellent chairman and colleagues. He proposed a toast to their chairman.

There followed a general rush for the boat. Elated and sated, the party from London left the Isle of Wight to resume its routine existence, and to muse on a fact that no one had mentioned: the staggering cost of the exercise. 'It will doubtless be many years,' the *Observer* remarked, 'before the shareholders in this undertaking will reap any reward for their outlay.' Events would one day confirm the towering truth of that prophecy. And within six weeks, on 28 August 1882, having succumbed to pneumonia, Henry Freeman was dead.

3

Mr Croydon

A glorious band, the chosen few.

Reginald Heber (1783–1826)

The Balfours had started their married life in Reigate: but even at twenty-five, Jabez was too big for Reigate. He needed a bigger stage. And so, early in 1869, he and Ellen packed up their first marital home and moved with their children to Croydon. Their daughter, named Clara Lucas Balfour Balfour so that the Balfour in her name should not be lost if and when she married, had been born in April 1867, just ten months after their wedding: Jabez never believed in hanging about. Their son James was born in May the following year. They moved first to a relatively modest house, Wilton Lodge, Broad Green, on the main road running from Croydon north to the village of Thornton Heath. As an optimist determined to make his name in the world, he no doubt saw this decent but far from grand address as merely a stepping stone.

Victorian Britain – especially Liberal Victorian Britain, to which Jabez from his early years subscribed – had few more cherished beliefs than its faith in progress. And Croydonians at this time, looking around their rapidly changing town, could be confident that few places in England embodied progress as richly as theirs did. In 1801, Croydon had been a modest settlement, with a population just short of 6,000. By 1851, that had more than tripled to 20,000; by 1871, two years after the Balfours arrived, it had all but tripled again, to 55,000; by the time Jabez moved on fifteen years later it had topped 100,000.

These were years when pride in the past began to take second place to pride in the future. Year after year, the preface of *Ward's Guide to Croydon* had begun with the words: 'Croydon is a town of great antiquity'. But the years of Croydon's expansion and Jabez's civic ascendancy changed all that, and *Ward's Guide* in time responded. 'Besides possessing other and more legitimate claims to importance,' the 1885 preface began, 'Croydon is a town of great antiquity'.

How buoyant they were at this moment, how self-confident, how full of congratulations and thanks to themselves and their colleagues; also of course to God, who had made such an enlargement of Croydon possible. When the town achieved borough status in 1883 its leading citizens could hardly contain their joy. London, it was agreed, was a mightier size than Croydon, but Croydon was growing mightily: were it not for the Surrey hills, it was noted, the town's southern expansion would soon touch on Merstham, Redhill and Reigate. But the size of a place was not the only test of its reputation. Did Croydon, when one assessed all its legitimate claims to esteem, deserve less admiration than London? Croydon, Jabez would tell the great banquet called to mark its achievement of municipal independence, was as old as the metropolis itself, and could boast of a history and local traditions as old as the City of London. Was it not remarkable, too, that while London, its powerful neighbour, had swallowed so much of what lay near to it, Croydon had maintained its separate local life?

But that independence was still far off when Jabez and Ellen arrived from Reigate with the children Clara and James. At present, Croydon was still part of Surrey, and forced in significant matters to bow its knee to the county's will. Meanwhile, there was valuable work to be done, institutions to be developed and shaped for the greater glory of Croydon. However great the claims of his other interests, Jabez was eager to throw himself into all the opportunities Croydon offered. This was a man who could not pass a fire without wanting to put an iron in it. He enlisted in the East Surrey volunteer regiment as a sub-lieutenant, rising to captain and then to major. 'The first officer to take a detachment under canvas,' the always admiring Liberal *Croydon Advertiser* said of him when he marched his troops back from Aldershot in the spring of 1875.

Jabez earned a reputation for public benefactions; to the Congregational Church of which he became a pillar, to hospitals, to schools, to the working men's club, to the temperance movement, indeed to most deserving causes that appealed for his charity. As a businessman closely watched and mostly admired in the City, and also a devout church attender, he could perhaps scarcely do otherwise; though he often did good by stealth, surreptitiously helping out deserving people whose case he had tried as a magistrate. When the Congregationalists built a new church in West Croydon (the building is still there, but is now a Jain temple) Jabez gave £1,000 towards it, and a peal of bells.

As a man of growing local eminence, he was soon found a place on the magistrates' bench, where his stated aim was to blend justice with understanding. It was not enough to fine the drunkard and send him away with a solemn instruction not to get drunk again. Such offenders must be brought under the kind of beneficial influence which would cause them to change their ways; for which purpose he, the vicar of Croydon and others resolved to set up a committee and hire a missionary. His life was already full of committees, from the Croydon General Hospital to the local branch of the Commons Preservation Society, which prevailed on him to be treasurer. When in 1881 a committee was established 'to bring university teaching within the reach of the inhabitants of Croydon of all classes and both sexes', the third name on the letterhead, after the Archbishop of Canterbury, president, and the headmaster of Whitgift School, chairman, was that of J. Spencer Balfour, treasurer. In later, unhappier times the *Pall Mall Gazette* would evoke his effortless rise to a dominant role in the life of the town. 'Evidently,' it recalled, 'he was the coming man, and there appeared to be no bounds to his popularity. He was afflu-ent, always smiling, always ready to give freely of both time and money.'

Beyond all that, as he documented years later in *My Prison Life*, 'I became, rather to my surprise, a prominent local politi-cian'. However, the evidence suggests that soon after he settled in Croydon he began to scheme his way towards a second career, at Westminster, preferably as Croydon's MP. He began, as many aspiring politicians did in those days, by standing in the school board elections. At his first attempt, in 1873, just five years after his arrival in Croydon, he topped the poll with 5,086 votes to the runner-up's 4,252. He was regularly re-elected thereafter, always outpolling the field.

As long as he could remember, Jabez had been a Liberal – as were most of the prominent non-conformists of the day. The continuing trial of strength in Croydon was between Anglican Conservatism and Liberal non-conformity. The clamour for Croydon's independence on the Liberal side had a hard political calculation embedded within its appeal to local pride; many rate-payers excluded from voting under the old vestry system would be given the vote if Croydon became a self-governing borough. Events proved them right. 'In Croydon,' says J. N. Morris in his history of religion and politics in the town, *Religion and Urban Change*, 'incorporation in 1883 put an end to the claims of Anglicanism to act as the focus of community loyalties . . . what the "democratisation" of local government . . . achieved therefore was the supersession of the Anglican oligarchy who had previously ruled the town by what was in effect "a new municipal elite".'

Party as well as personal ambition put Jabez in the thick of the fight. 'A sincere, thorough and hearty Liberal,' he called himself when he sought the party nomination at Tamworth in 1880. If asked to define his Liberalism, he told one party audience, he would say that its basis was trust and confidence in the people. Its purpose should be not just to secure their well-being, but to see that this was achieved with the people's own participation. Government ought to mean government by the whole of the people for the benefit of the whole of the people, as expressed through their party institutions.

Croydon's Liberals, no doubt in salute to his wealth as well as to his faith and his talent, installed him as president. 'He has infused new life into the Liberal Party,' wrote the *Advertiser*, 'and in this capacity, by his unusual courtesy, he has earned the admiration of the higher class of Conservatives who are not actuated by petty jealousy and private prejudice.' This claim had some justification. Even the Conservative *Croydon Review* saluted the value of J. Spencer Balfour, JP, MP, to the town's interests: 'A man,' it enthused, 'of wonderful business ability and of unusual capacity for chairing meetings.'

By this time it was always J. Spencer Balfour, never Jabez. He was J. Spencer Balfour both when strutting the streets of Croydon and when sitting on the Liberal benches at Westminster as MP for Tamworth, a seat he gained, as we shall see, in somewhat dubious circumstances. This preference for the second name over the first was popular in Victorian England – if often had a grander ring to it. There was nothing much wrong at this time with being called Jabez (though after his fall the name would come to be spurned). There were eminent Jabezes around, such as Jabez Bunting, 'the Methodist pope'. But once a man had come to be seen as Mr Croydon, as Jabez had by the end of the 1870s, something with rather more swagger seemed justified.

He had outgrown his house as well as his name. Some time around the end of 1879, he left Wilton Lodge. For the past five years his family had been scattered around the northern end of the town. He had moved his elderly parents to Thornton Heath; his brothers James and John had cottages in the area. His new home was one of the best addresses in town, a 'handsome and ancient mansion' called Wellesley House, just south of West Croydon station. This was a place where he could entertain in appropriate style. His doors, or at least his garden gates, were regularly thrown open for great local occasions. The Croydon Horticultural Society (whose president, the Archbishop of Canterbury, had a summer home at Addington Palace in Croydon and could therefore be persuaded to involve himself in many Croydon occasions) held its annual show under Jabez's trees among Jabez's shrubs and flowers.

His mother, who had nursed such hopes and such fears for him, was denied a sight of these glories: she never saw Wellesley House or her son's election to Parliament. Clara died in 1878 at the age of sixty-nine, much honoured and celebrated throughout the temperance movement and beyond. And soon afterwards, Ellen, his wife, also fades from the story. Accounts of his progress, reports of the great occasions which he addressed, sometimes mention his children, but never his wife. What had become of her? The explanation appears only in documents drawn up at his later bankruptcy, which explain that a trust fund was set up for her. Her mental health had declined to a point where in 1880 she was admitted to the Priory Hospital at Roehampton – an institution famous now for its treatment of troubled celebrities. She remained in care for the rest of her life. Jabez's son James was also away for much of the period from 1881 to 1883, at Uppingham public school. Though Jabez does not seem to have shown it, Ellen's distressing condition must have cast a shadow over what at this time was otherwise an exceptionally sunlit life.

4

J. Spencer Balfour, JP, MP

Forward! Be our watchword

Henry Alford (1810–71)

Towards the end of his life, Jabez Spencer Balfour wrote a short account of his Westminster career. It began like this, he said: in 1879, with an election approaching at which Mr Gladstone's Liberals were determined to evict the Tories, the Liberal chief whip approached him and asked if he would stand at Northampton alongside Charles Bradlaugh, the Radical Liberal and pamphleteer, who was later expelled from the Commons because as an atheist he refused to swear the oath of allegiance. Northampton, the chief whip explained, was a town which should have been won by the Liberals at the previous election but had fallen to the enemy, and candidates of high calibre were needed to take it.

Jabez visited the constituency and heard Bradlaugh speak. 'A better open air speech,' he recalled, 'I have never heard in my life.' His views, as a staunch non-conformist Christian, were very different from Bradlaugh's, but he saw him as an earnest political thinker and a born leader of men. Yet in the end, he declined to stand for Northampton, since the Liberals of Tamworth, on the boundary of Staffordshire and Warwickshire, had persuaded him to stand there instead. Even so, he had savoured his taste of Northampton: 'the pleasantest two hours I ever enjoyed in my life was with him [Bradlaugh] and Mr Labouchere' (another prominent radical Liberal, journalist and mischief-maker); this in a railway carriage returning from a banquet in Northampton.

The truth was different. That the suggestion had come out of the blue from the Liberal chief whip, W. P. Adam, is doubtful to say the least. Something – Jabez's record of business acumen, his work for the Liberals, the likelihood that he might provide financial aid to the party – may have caught Adam's eye. But the probability is that Jabez had, as we say nowadays, been networking – an art for which he had an indisputable talent. What is clearly false is the picture of Jabez being dragged towards various political altars by clamorous local Liberal parties eager to get their hands on him, and succumbing in the end to the wiles of Tamworth. In fact, he had carefully plotted to land the Liberal nomination there, even installing his elder brother John in the area to further his chances. John was put in charge of Jabez's mine at Hockley Hall, together with another at Whateley and a brickworks near Tamworth in March 1876, but the brothers also agreed, as John later recorded, that he should do all he could to 'make a seat in parliament for him at Tamworth'.

The financial return he expected only partly explained John's readiness to accept this subordinate role to a dominating brother twelve years his junior. Leaving Croydon would also give him a chance to emerge from Jabez's shadow. Their mother

Clara, now also living in Croydon, was sorry that he would be moving so far away but understood why he wished to do so. 'Croydon,' she wrote, 'has not been a lucky place to you and it has always seemed (judging by myself) that it added to your troubles being under the nose of the more prosperous – not better – members of the family.' John duly arrived in Tamworth, took over Jabez's interests, and began to cultivate local Liberal society. Presumably to disguise what he was doing, he initially dropped the name of Balfour, introducing himself as John Lucas.

The state of the Liberal party in the constituency was ideal for a contender with Jabez's radical views. Tamworth returned two members to parliament. The incumbent MPs were Sir Robert Peel, 3rd baronet, son of the Robert Peel who became prime minister and split the Conservative party over free trade, and a brewer called Hamar Bass. Peel was a forceful speaker, though the impact of his speeches in parliament owed something to the support of a clique that had gathered around him, applauding him noisily and laughing uproariously at the baronet's jokes whether they were truly funny or not.

Peel was also famously unreliable and capricious, and was busily dissipating the family fortunes by his wanton extravagance. He consistently failed to turn up for important constituency meetings. Worst of all for Tamworth Liberals, and especially for Tamworth Radical Liberals, he had regularly through the last parliament voted against his own party. Local Liberals, the *Tamworth Herald* reported in September 1879, were trying to find a more 'advanced' (that is, radical) member than either Peel or Bass to run at the coming election.

'Upon a cover of withered leaves, crisped by the frost, that sign of a mournful response to its feeble breathings,' the *Herald* wrote three months later, 'the old year lies dying, a dethroned king, with his successor waiting to pass the portals of life as he is clasped in the embrace of Death, and consigned to the past.' It was now 1880, the year of Jabez's opportunity. Peel had read the signs and saw that his time was up. When the dissolution of Parliament was announced in March, he declared that he would not be standing. A delegation from the more conservative wing of the local Liberal party did its best to change his mind. Even now, they hoped to avoid the expense and disruption of a contested election by finding a replacement candidate whom most of the town's 2,300 electors could back. Their choice was another brewer – W. H. Worthington, mayor of Burton-on-Trent. True, Worthington was a Conservative, but he said he was ready to run as a Liberal-Conservative.

But already, as the *Herald* reported, another contender was in the field – Jabez Spencer Balfour: 'a wealthy, charitable, shrewd, painstaking and thoroughly conscientious man, who is highly respected and honoured by those amongst whom he resides'. 'Mr Balfour,' it went on to disclose 'is a son of the late Mrs Clara Lucas Balfour, a lady whose philanthropic spirit and noble-hearted charity have been exemplified in numerous instances and whose voice and pen have frequently been most successfully applied in the cause of suffering humanity... He is said to possess great capacity as a businessman, and to display considerable facility and power in enunciating his views.'

As always, Jabez closed in on his opportunity with impressive speed. Sir Robert delivered his sad news on Wednesday; on Thursday Jabez was enunciating his views in an election address from his base at Hockley Hall.

> To the electors of Tamworth: Parliament being about to
> be Dissolved, and the Rt Hon Sir Robert Peel having
> issued a farewell address to his Constituents, I beg to
> offer myself as a Candidate for your suffrages. Being
> connected with the great mineral industries which have
> added so largely to the wealth and population of your
> district, my personal interests are identical with yours,
> and I may, therefore, be trusted to promote in every way
> the prosperity of your Borough. As a thorough Liberal in
> politics, I shall seek with unremitting zeal to promote
> the ascendancy of Liberal principles, and the return to
> power of a Liberal Administration, which will resume
> the great work of useful Domestic Legislation, which has
> been so much neglected by the present Government.
> Having lived among the industrial classes, I am in hearty
> sympathy with their views and aims, and I shall be
> prepared to support every well-considered measure to
> lighten their burden and improve their condition. I shall
> take an early opportunity of placing my views at length
> before you, and meanwhile remain
> Your very faithful servant
> J. Spencer Balfour
> Hockley Hall, Tamworth, March 10 1880.

A curious three-way contest ensued for the two Tamworth seats, with Bass remaining stiffly neutral between his fellow Liberal Balfour and his fellow brewer Worthington, now running as a Conservative while declaring his unwavering fidelity to Liberal principles. Despite Hockley Hall, Jabez was an outsider. 'His acquaintance with this district', said the not-unfriendly *Herald* 'is somewhat limited.' His appearance at his first meeting at Tamworth town hall was greeted with cries of 'what about Northampton?' The *Daily News*, he retorted, had alleged that he had sought nomination at Northampton. That was untrue. He had gone there simply to promote the cause of Liberal unity. True, the meeting there had passed a motion asking him to stand, with only two hands raised against it, and yes, he had agreed to think it over. But that was no more than a courtesy. Nothing was going to dissuade him from being part of a Bass–Balfour platform at Tamworth.

Worthington, at a rival meeting, continued to declare his attachment to Liberalism. But a questioner from the floor soon had him in trouble. Would this so-called Liberal support a motion of no confidence in the foreign policy of the Conservative government? 'No,' replied Worthington with self-lacerating candour, 'because I agree with them on that.' That answer alone, somebody signing himself 'A Lover of Progress' wrote to the *Herald*, disqualified him from representing Tamworth as a Liberal.

As the campaign developed exchanges grew rougher. At one meeting, supporters of Worthington prevented Jabez getting a hearing: in retaliation, Balfour supporters tried to overturn a wagon that Worthington had stood upon to speak. Balfour, the brewer's supporters charged, was a temperance man, an enemy of the Church of England, and a friend to the atheist Bradlaugh. 'Working men!' said one pamphlet circulated through the town, 'you don't want teetotalism forced on you. Churchmen: support your religion. And all of you: vote for Worthington.'

But they didn't. Tamworth voted on 3 April 1880. The mayor, Mr T. Cooke Jnr, announced the result amidst boisterous scenes at Tamworth town hall. Bass had topped the poll with 1,409 votes, making him the senior member for the constituency. Jabez had taken 1,074, putting him well ahead of the Liberal-Conservative and installing him as junior member for Tamworth. 'In his surprise and vexation,' he later recalled, 'he (my opponent) had stolen behind one of the great outer doors and was in danger of being nearly flattened to death as the shouting and groaning crowd of excited partisans poured after the mayor to the top of the outer stairs where, in accordance with immemorial practices, the result was proclaimed. Right in front stood the Burton town band, drawn up in gorgeous array, brought there to escort my opponent to the committee room to the strains of "Hail the Conquering Hero".' Instead it was Jabez who proceeded in triumph to the Castle Hotel, where he and Bass, together at last, addressed the exuberant crowd from the window. At thirty-six, Jabez was now entitled to call himself J. Spencer Balfour JP, MP.

Jabez came into the House of Commons on a Liberal tide

which, much to Queen Victoria's alarm, meant the return of Gladstone to the premiership. His cabinet appeared to confirm her worst fears: 'very radical', she gasped, though in fact it wasn't. Gladstone had picked six peers in a cabinet of fourteen, and old Whigs took most of the seats, leaving room at most for three radicals.

The new Parliament got off to the worst possible start with the long dispute over Bradlaugh's admission when the man who might have had Jabez as running mate refused to swear the oath and demanded that he be allowed to affirm. After much prevarication, the Commons expelled him. Thereafter proceedings were constantly disrupted by the obstructionist tactics of Irish MPs. The Liberals started with 352 seats, the Conservatives with 237 and the Irish Nationalists with 63, but the government made little use of its majority and was plagued by revolts. The new MP for Tamworth, not least because he hoped for office one day, was a Gladstone loyalist. Croydon, more even than Tamworth, had high hopes for him. 'Mr Balfour is a rising Liberal, and with his literary and oratorical abilities he will doubtless become a prominent member of the new Parliament,' enthused the *Norwood Review and Crystal Palace Reporter*.

Similar hopes were expressed when directors of the Croydon Tramways Company met for a celebratory lunch at The Ship in Greenwich. The company, declared his faithful Croydonian henchman Coldwells, owed everything to its chairman's tact and ability. Henry Freeman, the saviour of the Brading Harbour scheme, proposed a toast to him to which the chairman replied with 'a characteristically humorous speech'. At another celebratory lunch, the usual Balfour Group gang were there in force: S. R. Pattison, chairman of the Liberator, George Brock and Coldwells from Croydon, Henry Freeman, and on this occasion a younger recruit to the Balfour hierarchy, his nephew Leonard Balfour Burns, son of Jabez's sister Cecil and the Revd Dawson Burns. But other City dignitaries, not on Jabez's payroll, had also come to pay their respects, among them the master of the Worshipful Company of Fan Makers, of which Jabez was Warden that year.

Throughout his political life Jabez was always in demand to speak in his colleagues' campaigns, especially at elections. He knew how to cajole and flatter and entertain and finally sway an audience. Yet his famous loquacity largely deserted him in the House. He rarely spoke: what the always supportive *Advertiser* back in Croydon saluted as his acclaimed maiden speech was in fact just a question about the failure of the water supply during a rescue operation at a fire in north Woolwich. Like the town's senior member, Hamar Bass, he took the view that most MPs spoke too often. Better to spend one's time being useful behind the scenes, in committee, or pressing the cases brought by constituency deputations.

Hard work was what counted. 'Before I went to parliament, I thought I was tolerably conversant with the duties,' he declared at one dinner in proposing a toast, the fifth of twelve in the course of the evening, to the mayor, aldermen and councillors of Tamworth. 'But the very short experience I have had has shown me that I was as ignorant as the most ignorant could be of the amount of work devolving on a member of parliament.'

He and his friend Hamar Bass, he declared to applause, were never in a hurry to get away from the Commons, and always ready to endure the late-night sittings which parliamentary life was forcing upon them. Occasions like these were invaluable: together with party meetings, handing out prizes at schools, occasional kindly benefactions and conspicuous hospitality they helped keep his name before the Tamworth public.

And yet there was always a sense in which, while representing Tamworth, he was also already member for Croydon. Delegations from Tamworth were invited to Croydon and ripely entertained. The Tamworth military volunteers visited those of Croydon. Croydon was left in no doubt that his presence at Westminster as member for Tamworth was helping to bring the town ever closer to the borough status, independent of imperious Surrey, that it longed for. 'I never forgot I was a Croydon man,' he told yet another approving gathering in the town's Greyhound Hotel. 'Croydon was never out of my mind, and I have remembered, as you no doubt do, that Croydon ought to have a member of Parliament. Until it has, be kind enough to look upon me, as long as I have a seat in Parliament, as member for Croydon – always remembering, however, that I must make the interests of my constituency at Tamworth my first consideration. I can say of Croydon that –

> Where'er I roam.
> Whatever lands I see,
> My heart, untravelled
> Fondly turns to thee.'

The Tamworth constituency was due to disappear in a reorganization of seats for the next election. Once, giving evidence to a Commons committee, Jabez had inadvertently introduced himself as the member for Croydon. That was clearly what he now intended to be.

Though Jabez came happily out of his Tamworth adventure, his brother John, who had worked so hard to put him there, did not. Soon after Jabez took his seat a quarrel began which developed into outright hostility and led to a long estrangement between them. On 1 May 1881, on the notepaper of the Hockley Hall and Whateley Collieries and Brick Works Ltd, John wrote a memorandum, to be read by his wife and family 'in case I should die suddenly', setting out how things stood between him and his brother. In the course of it he recounted a fierce argument a few days before during which he had challenged Jabez about the way things were managed at the Liberator and the House and Lands Investment Trust and had questioned the sums the directors were paying themselves. He was all the more alarmed, he recorded, because Jabez had been talking openly of the troubles affecting one of his companies, and referring to its possible ruin. Jabez had even hinted that he might be ready to leave the country, because he was 'sick of it'.

John was adamant that Jabez had failed to honour the agreement made between them when he left Croydon for Tamworth – that Jabez would pay him to act as his manager and agent – and for years that dispute remained unresolved. There was further trouble after old Jimmy Balfour's death in December

1884, extending this time to their brother James and their sister Cecil and her husband Dawson Burns. Documents now came to light which John and his brother James found baffling. Why had Dawson, as the records appeared to show, been entrusted with so much of their father's holdings in the Liberator? And why had sums of money then been drawn out apparently without Dawson's consent? 'They seem,' James wrote to John, 'to have a very slipshod way of treating these things at the Liberator.' Jabez, when asked to explain, was affronted, especially by the terms of a letter (which has not survived) from Cecil. Some of her comments about him, Jabez complained, were 'libellous'. Dawson responded on her behalf next day. If anything here was libellous, he insisted, it was the implications of remarks that Jabez had made about him.

All that blew over. Dawson, having investigated, said nothing untoward had occurred. But it demonstrated that family suspicions about Jabez's dealings were by no means confined to John. Meanwhile the animosity between John and Jabez persisted. If the correspondence that has survived is representative, then Jabez emerges from their later exchanges as little less than a monster.

The core of the trouble was this. Jabez had turned the Hockley Hall operation into a public company. For the first time in ten years its results were properly audited. This led to a dispute over the terms on which John had been employed. He had an arrangement with Jabez to be paid £1,000 a year, together with reasonable expenses and a bonus for success. But no formal contract had been drawn up, and the auditors were now questioning the money that John was drawing. Far from getting too little, as he often complained, John, they suspected, had been getting too much.

When John wrote to Jabez complaining about what he saw as an unjustified slight, he at first got no answer. When he persisted, a letter arrived, dated 1 September 1887, which portrays a side of Jabez he mostly kept from the world – though his subordinates knew it only too well. Why had he not replied? Because, Jabez said, he was so overwhelmed with shame that his brother should have put himself in this dreadful position, and without even offering Jabez the chance to save him. 'Professing to be a poor man,' he wrote, 'you have always asked for recognition of your pluck and devotion in sticking to your work for so small a pittance, whereas you have actually been helping yourself systematically to a very large income. I can do nothing now, and the ridiculous and blustering way in which you have treated the affair has naturally incensed everyone against you. I have done all I can do and must now stand aside. You will be prosecuted and in Tamworth! And our name so honourably connected with the place will be dragged through the mire and your unfortunate children, who have been going to and fro about the place for years, will feel the whole weight of this dreadful blow. Your betrayed and unhappy bro – JSB.'

John replied by return. This letter, he said, appalled him. He recalled the promises he believed that Jabez had made to him when he first went to Tamworth, and his proven success in running the businesses. To enhance Jabez's chances of winning the Tamworth nomination, he had been forced at some cost to masquerade before local Liberals as a man of means, and acquire a house suitable for that station. 'When you lost your seat,' he chided his brother, 'you never looked this way and dropped the lot of us and now seek to ruin me . . . I have been too much your slave. You have thought fit to order me as you like and I fool-like have allowed it.'

The response next day from Jabez was merciless. 'If anything were wanted to add to the baseness of your conduct,' he wrote, 'it would be supplied by this communication in which you tell me that I "seek to ruin you" whereas I only heard of your frauds a few days ago and have since then taken no part in the proceedings against you . . . As regards my connection with Tamworth, the figures show that your embezzlements commenced long before I dreamt of standing for Tamworth . . . Your embezzlements have continued up to the present year though you are base enough to declare that since I lost the seat I have "dropped the lot of you". Ask your own sons and daughters if I have dropped them . . . Having said this I decline any further communication with you . . . '

It took the intervention of a senior Liberator figure the following month to quell the brothers' wrangling. Jabez's ban on further communications continued until July 1891, when John defied it to alert his brother to a problem affecting Jabez's interests in Tamworth. Jabez's response, in a letter he ended with his old formula, 'affectionately yours', seemed on the surface ready for compromise. 'It has been a mystery to me,' he wrote, 'how you could think unkindly and harshly of me, and if

I have erred towards you it has been inadvertently.' John responded in a letter whose opening used Jabez's childhood nickname: 'Dear Ja-Ja...' But the letter was stern. There had, he reminded his brother, been that accusation of embezzling; and he still had not got the money he thought he deserved. There was nothing to be gained, Jabez wrote in reply, from raking over the past. 'I can only repeat and I say it solemnly as in the sight of God that I have never meant to wrong you and I don't think I have done so. If I had, you surely know me well enough to know that I would own my fault to you frankly and unreservedly.' If John would only read his former letters again, Jabez insisted, he would surely understand how hurtful they had been.

It was as if the allegations that John had embezzled the company's money and those gloating forecasts of John's coming disgrace had never been. 'I only wish...I had your gift of erasure,' John wrote back. Jabez, once more, was unyielding. The dispute over money that John said he was owed could be swiftly resolved, he said. But there could be no reconciliation between them until John withdrew the wounding things he had said in earlier letters. Nor could he deal with John's griev-ances in any fraternal spirit unless this was done. It would have to be left to lawyers. 'Anyhow God bless you,' Jabez ended a further letter, 'and if you don't regret your letters that only makes my regret the deeper.'

Two days later he wrote again, demanding the retraction of John's earlier letters even more strongly: 'Their language', he said, 'is so extravagant that I should have thought you would have been happy to have them destroyed.' In the end, though, Jabez withdrew his demand and agreed to a meeting at which they settled their business dispute. The form of words that embodied the deal was not agreed until January 1892 – only months before Jabez got his own painful taste of having the good name of Balfour dragged through the mire.

5

His Worship the Mayor

Hark, those bursts of acclamation!
Hark, those loud triumphant chords!

Thomas Kelly (1769–1855)

Let us consider Jabez on a sunny spring morning some time in 1883, at ease, perhaps with a cigar in his hand, at the window of his headquarters at Budge Row in the City. He stands with his feet apart, stocky, and growing stout. In later, less kindly times some will call him a dwarf, though he is at least 5 feet 4 inches. Some say he resembles Napoleon, a comparison he may not altogether resent. He is, in every sense, a very substantial figure: 'Balfour the prosperous financier, the temperance enthusiast, the pious and trusted man, the darling of the City, the rising parliamentarian,' as one newspaper described him as he was in the days of his eminence.

If he looks pleased with life, no wonder. This autumn he is going to be forty and, with all appropriate modesty, he has done pretty well. His dear mother has been dead five years, but his father survives: he will turn eighty-seven in October. Ellen's mental deterioration is sad, but she is well cared for at the Priory. His children are a consolation: Clara, sixteen in 1883, is so bright and self-possessed; James continues his studies at Uppingham. Jabez's fine house and glorious garden at Croydon are much admired, and he has now added an imposing country address: the Manor House, Long Wittenham, not far from the Thames, south of Oxford.

The world can tell from the published results how his company network is thriving. True, he had a spot of bother with the auditors of the House and Lands Investment Trust in February, but that had been swiftly and sweetly dealt with by a brisk piece of chairmanship at the annual general meeting the following month. His portfolio of directorships is a matter for awe. These are not just Balfour companies either: indeed, he has begun to withdraw from his formal role at the head of some of them – even of his celebrated, trail-blazing building society – though as his colleagues would be first to say he remains his old commanding, all-conquering presence. And his magic touch is demonstrated each year by the swelling list of organizations eager to haul him on board: a catalogue which by now includes the Cambridge Street Tramways Company (chairman); Crooke's Mining and Smelting Company Limited; the Croydon Tramways Company (chairman); the House and Lands Investment Trust (chairman); the London and Lancashire Fire Insurance Company (London Board); the London, Edinburgh and Glasgow Assurance Company Limited; Mansion House Chambers, Limited; Metropolitan Mills, Limited; the National Model Dwellings Company Limited; Northampton Street Tramways Limited.

Down on the Isle of Wight, his embankment is still more

than holding its own with Neptune and the trains are running across it to Bembridge; his fine hotel looks serenely out over the Solent. Poor Freeman has gone, but reliable old Coldwells has come down from Croydon to take charge of the enterprise.

As befits a man who has made his mark on the city, Jabez has risen in 1881 to the highest office in the Worshipful Company of Fan Makers, succeeding Henry Freeman as Master: several past Masters have gone on to become sheriffs of the City of London, even Lord Mayors. And so many other boards and committees crowded into his life: the school board at Croydon, committees or governing boards of local hospitals, even – for Jabez prides himself on the breadth of his hinterland – a place on the committee of the Surrey County Cricket Club at the Oval. That was one of his many clubs, along with the Reform, the Devonshire, the National Liberal (of which he was a founder member). He was a fellow, too, of the Royal Statistical Society. As he strolled about London, this was a man whom many people of eminence recognized and nodded to, even engaged in jovial conversation.

Perhaps, at forty, he should have pushed ahead with his other career in politics? Nevertheless his diligence and loyalty on the back-benches, not to mention his financial gifts to his party, must have impressed the party hierarchy. The coming redistribution of seats would see the elimination of Tamworth as a separate constituency, but for a man with such responsibilities in the City and in Croydon, a seat on the far side of Birmingham was less than ideal in any case. To be elected for Croydon itself would be perfect. Even some of the

Conservative papers admitted the benefits he had brought to the town. And to cap it all, on 15 February 1883 the Privy Council gave draft approval to a charter bestowing borough status on Croydon. Jabez, of course, was one of the first to know, and sent his butler to break the glad news to the colloquy known as the Croydon House of Commons, where matters of national importance were debated.

Recollected many years after – though in confinement, rather than tranquillity – this was perhaps the best time of Jabez's life. By March there was fevered speculation in Croydon as to who would emerge as the town's charter mayor. The decision would be made by the council, on which, if the coming elections went according to plan, there would be plenty of Balfour trusties, including George Brock, Frank Coldwells and the builder J. W. Hobbs. Jabez himself had never stood for the council and saw no need to do so now.

By 10 May, at a public reception for the charter, he was clearly way ahead of the field. It was he who proposed the principal toast of the evening – to Croydon – on an evening which epitomized the municipal pride that flourished in late Victorian England. A procession bearing the charter from a flag-draped West Croydon station through festive streets to the Greyhound Hotel, very artistically decorated and arranged for the occasion under the direction of Mr A. C. Ebbutt; then a sumptuous seven-course banquet for a company of 125. Ten toasts, occasioning twenty speeches – three by the chairman, none other than J. Spencer Balfour, MP, who expressed his hope that a year from now such speeches would be made not by a humble individual like him (cries of No, No) but by a fully-fledged mayor. All interspersed with songs ('A Warrior Bold', Mr Bantock Pierpoint; 'He Thinks I Do Not Love Him', Madame Henrietta Whyte). No ladies were present, apart from those invited to sing.

These were men who had built a fine town by their own endeavour, the envy of lesser neighbours. Though governments imposed certain constraints upon them, they could feel that Croydon's destiny was now in their own hands, and they meant to advertise that fact to the world. They looked at the old town hall – not in truth, very old; it had only been there since 1809 – and agreed that it would not do. Something bigger and much more appropriate to the town's importance would have to be built. The old, dependent era was over. No one caught this mood better all evening than Jabez.

On 9 June Jabez was approved as mayor by a vote of 23 to 10. He took the chair in the council chamber to loud applause ('mingled,' the Conservative *Croydon Chronicle* reported with some satisfaction, 'with a certain amount of hissing'). His elevation called for a grand garden party – at which Clara, in her mother's absence, acted as hostess – 'who with an ease and grace beyond her years made the party very pleasant and enjoyable'. And, of course, a further banquet was essential, with his fellow MP Hamar Bass, the mayor, a dozen councillors and the vicar arriving by special train from Tamworth to do honour to their MP. Had they gone all over England, Bass told them with a generosity he had not always shown Jabez, they could not have chosen a man with greater business capacities. In July, as if to demonstrate that the old causes had not been deserted in the midst of all this banqueting, Jabez staged a temperance party under the trees at Wellesley House where the mineral waters of Messrs Peckham and Co. were found very acceptable.

The mayors of the 1880s were more like the new-look mayors of the early twenty-first century were intended to be: town leaders, setting the pace and taking a firm executive role. Jabez revelled in the whole of it, the entertaining and the decision-making alike. Warm tributes were paid on all sides to the fairness and effectiveness of his chairmanship. When his first term ended in November, the council, led by one of his fiercest opponents in the vote in June, prevailed upon him to stay for a second term.

Yet 1884 never quite matched the triumphs of 1883. At the start of the year while in Rome he picked up an illness which caused him to miss every council meeting until April, when he reappeared to a thunderous ovation by which he seemed overwhelmed. At the end of the year, three days before Christmas, his father died at eighty-eight, and was buried in Paddington Old Cemetery alongside the wife he had lost six years before. And during his second term as mayor Jabez made new political enemies. Part of the trouble arose from the state of the tramway company, set up on his initiative and now, as the system reached completion, far from successful. It had debts, his opponents complained, of £203,000, reflecting the extravagance with which its affairs were conducted; its costs, at £15,600 a mile, were way above those for any other tramway in England. By now, Jabez had left the company, but that did not spare him the blame. Soon it was in receivership, with investors losing everything they had put into it.

Perhaps more damaging still was his opposition in Parliament to a bill to bring a new railway to Croydon. Even political allies distrusted his motives here. Among his financial interests, which spread far more widely than his many director-ships, was one in the London Brighton and South Coast Railway (LBSCR). Balfour and his associate Hobbs had been buying land in Streatham and Norwood which the LBSCR from London to Croydon could serve. The Balfour Group would gain no such advantage from the line that was now proposed from Dulwich through to South Croydon, and the LBSCR could expect to lose some of its passenger revenue to the interloper. For an ordinary LBSCR director to seek to banish the newcomers would be reasonable enough. For the mayor of Croydon to do so – however much he might have assured the parliamentary committee that he spoke in a purely personal capacity – was indefensible. 'You, sir,' Councillor Hinton reminded him, 'are located in a palatial residence in the centre of town.' The existing line ran close to his house. The people in train-starved South Croydon did not enjoy such privilege. A meeting of Croydon working men, chaired by a local Liberal, expressed 'deep indignation' over what Jabez had done. Resentment was also growing over the arrogance of Jabez's clique, who had taken to turning up on some occasions all wearing white hats, to signify their allegiance.

All this mattered much more because, though his term as mayor was now closing, he had a higher ambition – to represent Croydon in Parliament. The Gladstone government was becoming too weak to continue, and gave way in June 1885 to an interim Conservative administration. An election was not far off. In the book he published twenty years later, Jabez would maintain that when Croydon became a parliamentary borough, the leaders of his party had personally prevailed on him to contest the seat, as he was the only Liberal who could win it. What was more, he claimed, so great was his devotion to the cause of Liberal Croydon that he had turned down the chance of fighting a safe seat elsewhere to do so.

Whatever the truth of that, the Tories were clearly worried. The lawyer William Grantham, who had represented Croydon in the old Parliament as MP for East Surrey, was persuaded, despite his extreme reluctance (he had earlier ruled out any such possibility, as had the other incumbent, a Conservative brewer called Watney), to give up the chance of fighting the new safe Tory seat at Reigate and to take on Jabez instead. Grantham knew Balfour well: 'my friend and my parliamentary pair' he called him at one of the banquets that punctuated their lives. But the contest was brutal and bitter. The monthly *Croydon Review*, which had lavishly praised Jabez's mayoralty and treated him to an almost adoring profile, had warned that things would be different now. 'It would be a pity if, after such a successful mayoralty, the good feelings brought about should be sacrificed. If, however, he stands for Croydon, every effort must be made to show him that the Borough does not yet believe in Bradlaughism, blasphemy, or disestablishment.'

Even his opposition to the promised railway to Croydon took a poor second place to his long and well-established alignment with the Liberation Society – an organization, claimed Tories, hell bent on destroying the Church of England. He might be a regular worshipper at West Croydon Congregational Church, but support for the Liberation Society amounted, on their score sheet, almost to atheism. The very future of Christianity, Tories claimed, was at stake. 'If the religionists of Croydon have any respect for religion,' wrote the *Croydon Review*, 'if they do not want Christianity to become a matter of the past; if they are ready to do their little in supporting that for which their ancestors in centuries past have striven so hard to secure and maintain; if they wish their families to grow up under Christian influence, it is clearly their duty... not to vote for Mr Balfour.'

Other old charges resurfaced. The man was a Chartist. He favoured electing the second chamber and expelling hereditary peers (that was true). He threatened the working man's right to drink by backing the 'local option', allowing Croydon to vote on the opening of public houses. (So he did: but the Tory leader Lord Salisbury favoured that too.) 'Woe betide any government that tries to rob the poor man of his beer,' the chairman of the Croydon Licensed Victuallers told their annual dinner, to which both Balfour and Grantham sent apologies for their absence. Even one of the town's temperance groups counselled voting to stop him on the grounds that he was friendly to Bradlaugh.

Once Grantham was in the field, the odds were always

against Jabez winning Croydon in an election where England was swinging towards to the Tories. The vote that did for him took place on Saturday, 5 December 1885, with the polling booths open, under a new reform, until 8 p.m. rather than 4, so that even more drink than usual must have been taken by the time the votes were all counted. In this case, it wasn't till 12.15 the following morning that the returning officer was ready. Grantham, with 5,484, had taken 56 per cent of the vote, leaving the great Liberal hope with an ignominious 44 per cent (4,315). Returning home in his disappointment, Jabez found his peace further disturbed. Some hostile person – disavowed by the Tories – had arranged for the Dead March from Handel's *Saul* to be played outside Wellesley House.

Grantham's value to the Conservatives was emphasized when a month later he announced he was leaving Parliament, having been appointed a judge. He had never even taken his seat in the new House of Commons. Croydon seemed condemned to go through the whole electoral process again – but this time not just without Grantham but without J. Spencer Balfour as well.

Jabez did not intend to risk a further humiliation. From now on, the celebratory occasions in which he would once have taken a prominent place had to manage without him. Though the Croydon Horticultural Society still enjoyed the use of his grounds, he did not turn up for the mayor's reception for Grantham's successor, nor for the mayoral garden party in June. He no longer took his seat on the bench; he resigned from the Volunteers. He was far away when a new chairman revealed to the annual general meeting the 'melancholy' state of the tramways.

In April 1887 his daughter Clara was married at West Croydon Congregational Church by her uncle, the Revd Dawson Burns, to Walter Bishop, son of another prominent Croydon Liberal. He was thirty-one; she was nineteen. After that, Jabez finished with Croydon. The West End of London – Marlborough Gate, close to Hyde Park – was the place for a man of his prominence now. And he had another consolation as well: the life of a country squire in the Oxfordshire village of Burcot.

6

The Squire of Burcot

Full enjoyment,
Full, unmixed, and evermore.

Thomas Kelly (1769–1854)

The title of squire is not some kind of official appointment, or an honour formally bestowed, like a knighthood. It is more a mark of local respect, earned sometimes by benevolence, sometimes by intimidation. Jabez was squire of Burcot because he owned most of the village. For some time he had kept a house, almost certainly rented, at Long Wittenham, about three miles away. But Burcot was quite as handy for London – Culham station, an hour and twenty minutes from Paddington, was just down the road – and right on the Thames.

He bought Burcot House, with its boathouses and its island opposite in the Thames, late in 1886 or early in 1887, and gradually added to them the house next door – Burcot Grange with its paddocks, tower, cottage and stables – a farm, a stretch of land to the north of the village, a lodge, and half a dozen farmworkers' cottages. He also bought Queensford Mill in Dorchester, adding it to a portfolio of properties acquired over the years, owned not by his companies but by himself: these

included a farm on the Isle of Wight, near his mother's childhood home and a house and thirty-three acres at Gatton, near
the town of Reigate in Surrey where he had grown up.
Properties in Brighton, Derby, Tamworth, Doncaster and elsewhere would be settled in the trust fund for his wife, drawn up
in March 1892 when her illness had for some time been judged
incurable – and when, unknown to most of the world, the
future of his empire had begun to look seriously threatened.
But Burcot was his particular pride and the place where he
most wanted to be when not required in the City or at
Westminster.

He swiftly set about improving both the house and the
village. He gave the house an entirely new frontage ('the result',
the *Victoria History of the County of Oxford* would later
complain, 'was to destroy the symmetry and proportions of the
structure'), with an Italian garden laid out before it, and an
indoor tennis court to one side. This, like his grand new London
address at Marlborough Gate, Hyde Park, was a place in which
to entertain and to be admired, to demonstrate his legendary
generosity and the breadth of his taste. Up to twenty people
would come for a weekend. The great temperance advocate had
a lavish collection of fine wines at Burcot, as the police would
discover when they raided the place after he disappeared, taking
away fifty cases, including thirty-year-old clarets and twenty
different brands of high-class champagne. There were books –
his favourites were Dickens and Thackeray – and pictures (his
taste was described by those who knew more about it than he
did as 'undiscerning'), and swimming and boating, and tennis

even at night, since he'd had his indoor court fitted out with electricity, and whist and billiards. Jabez preferred, one old friend recalled, to watch others play billiards rather than play himself, which he did maladroitly. The same was true of his tennis: he played energetically, but not very well. He liked to treat his guests to recitations from Tennyson, though some found the chosen extracts rather too long. His staff were well looked after and treated to a sovereign each every Christmas. In his absence, the place was run by Rebecca Bishop, sister of the Walter Bishop who had married Jabez's daughter Clara in 1887.

In a millennium history of Clifton Hampden and Burcot published just after her death in 1999, Sheila Llewellyn reported the recollections of a pantry boy on Jabez's staff – twenty-first in the pecking order of the house's indoor servants – called Peter Tinson. Breakfasters at Burcot, Tinson recalled, would have ten or fifteen dishes to choose from: porridge, eggs, bacon, kidneys, kippers, cold fowl and York hams. As for the liquor, it used to take three carriages to deliver Jabez's orders. 'Later on,' according to Tinson, 'I used to wonder what some of the little ministers, living in their manses, with hardly two pennies to rub together, would think of all this luxury, which, in a way, they had provided. But you see he had a position to keep up, because at that time people thought of him as the successful British businessman.'

A walk around the village demonstrated that Jabez was not just a squire but a squire who reformed and improved. He tore down farmworkers' hovels and replaced them with sturdy high-quality cottages (selling, in the spring of 2003, suitably modernized and extended, for £250,000 at least and perhaps £375,000 for the best of them). A creditors' meeting after the crash was told that he had spent £5,000 on them. He gave the village gas lamps, and promised electricity, though he never got round to that. He established a village institute and encouraged the villagers to run it themselves. Parties were thrown for the whole village to come to and get a taste of the big house's hospitality: on the birthday, for instance, of his son James, now Captain Balfour, at which the gratified villagers presented James with a handsome sandwich case and a horn flask. 'Any person who takes the trouble to visit the neighbourhood,' Jabez wrote two decades later in *My Prison Life*, 'can ascertain the estimation in which, I am glad to learn, I am still held there.'

Burcot House, as Jabez knew it, has now gone. It passed from the private owners who succeeded Jabez after the crash to become in time a college for missionaries – in its final days, for Serbian missionaries. In 1954 H. G. (Bert) Mullard, a local businessman, bought it at auction, as Jabez had. He had called on a friend in Abingdon, heard of the auction, looked in, found no one was bidding, so did so himself. His wife knew nothing of this until he came home and said: 'I've bought Burcot House.' It was, he says, a surprisingly awkward, inconvenient house: despite Jabez's pride in his books and his hospitality, the library and dining room were badly proportioned. The most attractive part of the house were the third-floor attics where Jabez's servants lived. Mullard pulled it down and replaced it, though the tennis court, now used mainly for table tennis, survives.

The island in the Thames has gone too: it just disappeared, people say, during dredging by the Thames Conservancy.

There was much fine entertaining done at Burcot, and many compliments paid by gratified guests to their generous host. But the greatest public occasion of all, and the one that was most characteristic of J. Spencer Balfour, JP, MP, took place at Whitsun 1892, only five months before his world was turned upside down. This was the opening of the recreation ground with which he had presented the abbey village of Dorchester, just down the road. The parish magazine of July 1892 recorded this happy occasion in a way that recaptures an essential dimension of late Victorian Britain as little else can.

Whitsun Monday having been fixed upon by Mr Balfour for the opening of the Recreation Ground, which he has so generously set apart and laid out for the purpose on his land, the village was *en fête*. For some days previously, preparations and arrangements had been made by a village committee, under Mr Latham as chairman, with a view to showing Mr Balfour on the occasion an unmistakable evidence of the gratitude, which was felt by the people of the village, for the kindness he was going to show toward them. The committee, after sitting for some hours on the question, hatched a prodigiously large chicken, in the shape of a village procession, in which the various kinds of village life and occupation were to be represented. The programme would be as follows:

Watlington Nephalite Brass and Reed Band
Vicar and staff
Churchwarden, gravedigger, sexton and choir boys
Recreation Ground committee
Girls' School, headed by May Queen
Boys' School
Missionary College

Friendly societies:
Ancient Order of Foresters, Court Royal Oxonian No 5546
Dorchester Friendly Society
Hearts of Oak
Operative Bricklayers' Society
Berkshire Friendly Society
Jesters

Chimney sweep
Bootmakers
Hurdle Makers
Straw Drawers
Basket Makers
Maltsters
Engine Drivers
Postman
Gardeners and Cart of Flowers
Grooms, mounted
Tailor and Tailoress
Wheelwrights
Blacksmiths
Carpenters

Bricklayers and Labourers
Painters, Plumbers etc
Stonemasons
Asphalter, with furnaces on cart
Fisherman and Waterman
Laundresses in wagon
Carrier

Coal merchant
Stone hauliers
Miller, and load of flour
Land surveyor
Butcher with fat ox
Bakers with bread in cart
Grocers, with Chinaman and tea on van
Licensed Victuallers
Sport
Fire engine
Blacksmith, with anvil in cart
Farmer in smock frock
Plough with pair of horses
Drill
Horse hoe
Load of wheat
Wagon with winnowing machines and meal
Load of hay
Haymaker
Horse rake
Haymakers with wagon

Load of mangolds
Load of potatoes
Mares with foals

Jersey cow
Jersey bull
Shorthorn cow and calf
Milk cart
Sheep
Lambs
Poultry and ducks
Eggs and butter
Entire horses
Heavy presser
Van, with corn, small farm seeds, butter and eggs
Labourers and families
Cowboy (Mr C Hatt) on horse.

(A Nephalite band was one made up of temperance people. An entire horse is one that has not been castrated – that is, a stallion.)

'Never before in the memory of the oldest inhabitants,' the account continued 'had there been seen so many people in the village. A small proportion of the procession, consisting of the churchwardens, the vicar and his staff, the ground committee, and the schoolchildren followed the Band into the centre of the ground, where Mr Balfour was stationed in his carriage and with Mr and Mrs James Balfour and Miss Bishop.'

Mr Balfour called on the vicar to offer prayers. Mr Mackett

and Miss Smith then appeared to perform 'a short ode' commissioned for the occasion, with specially written music:

> We greet with truest welcome
>> Fair Burcot's squire today
> And for his generous bounty
>> Our hearty thanks we pay.
> His gift will sweeten labour,
>> At close of summer's day,
> 'Twill cheer all drooping spirits
>> And mirth and laughter weigh.
>
> Dull care shall hence be banished
>> Bold sport shall reign supreme:
> Here shall the maidens gather
>> To crown the May Day Queen;
> And new delight and vigour
>> This pleasure ground shall lend
> To cricket, race and football
>> As oft our youth contend.
>
> Here children's happy voices
>> Shall carol forth at play,
> Here, gaining health and vigour
>> Our men shall end the day.
> And as the years roll onward
>> This time we'll not forget
> When to praise the gift and giver
>> Both young and old were met.

Colonel Blunt then called for three cheers, 'which were most heartily given', the band striking up, 'For He's a Jolly Good Fellow'. The jolly good fellow now rose to great acclaim and asked the vicar to lead them in prayers. Once they were over, Mr Balfour delivered a lengthy speech, mostly a modest account of how the gift had come to be made. He expressed the hope that the match they were about to see (Mr Balfour's XI against a Surrey XI, which as a committee man he had been able to muster) would give them some excellent cricket. There were only two rules he would wish the villagers to apply. One, there must be no bad language; the other, there must be no gambling. 'I don't think villagers in this part of the world have so much money to spare,' he added, 'that they need indulge in the pleasures of gambling.'

Mr Balfour and his party then drove off amidst the cheers of all assembled, and the multitude of people (apart, presumably, from those who stayed to watch the cricket) gradually dispersed. Mr Balfour's XI made 130; the Surrey XI floundered at first and seemed likely to lose, but then rallied and won the game by five wickets. So ended a day, which just as Mr Mackett and Miss Smith had forecast, would never be forgotten by those who were there.

That was not, however, the end of the story. Later, after Jabez's empire had crashed and the Midas of Burcot had vanished, the Recreation Ground committee were surprised to receive a letter asking for unpaid rent. The land that J. Spencer Balfour had presented to the people of Dorchester was not in fact his to give. He had never bought it. No doubt he had meant to get round to it; but before he could do so, graver matters had intervened.

7

The Member for Burnley

Fading is the worldling's pleasure
All his boasted pomp and show

John Newton (1725–1807)

A mong those invited to taste the delights of Burcot were the members of the Burnley Literary and Scientific Club. Having resolved that their annual excursion should be to Oxford, they found themselves being reprogrammed, rather in the manner of Mr Toad of Toad Hall. The itinerary now read: steamer down the Thames from Oxford, organized by J. Spencer Balfour, MP. Luncheon at the Burcot home of J. Spencer Balfour. Visit to Sinodun Hill and Dorchester, followed by dinner at Burcot, hosted by J. Spencer Balfour. Principal speaker:...

One of those who went on this trip wrote an account of it that the Unionist *Burnley Express and Advertiser*, despite its steady denigration of Jabez, printed three weeks later. 'Very soon,' he wrote:

[we] were able to appreciate the characteristic beauty of the neighbourhood. The bright sunlight, unimpeded by

the smoke so familiar to Burnley people, shone on the
placid waters and the rich green foliage. At length,
Burcot, charmingly placed with its beautifully laid
out grounds, running down to the river, was reached.
Mr J. S. Balfour, MP, and his son and daughter received
the party on the lawn. Admiration was expressed of
the majestic trees which adorned the grounds and the
surpassing beauty of the situation. Lunch was partaken
of in a marquee which Mr Balfour had erected for the
accommodation of his numerous guests...'

When they got back from Dorchester in the evening they
found a sumptuous dinner awaiting them. Thanked for his
'princely hospitality', Mr Balfour said he felt an MP ought to
keep closely in touch with all his constituents, whatever their
political opinions. Although he might sometimes be depicted
as a villain of the deepest dye, he hoped that people might
learn that he was not as bad as he was represented, and that he
did not entertain the evil designs against the Church and the
empire with which he had been charged.

Nine months later the members of the Burnley Liberal
Association executive were given a comparable treat: being
fewer in number, they were invited to stay at Jabez's country
home for a couple of nights. On another occasion nine local
government representatives – 'including the delegate from the
rural sanitary authority' – were entertained not at Burcot but at
the Savoy, where Jabez had them served with a twelve-course
dinner, complete with jokes and stories, washed down with the

finest wines, which, according to one present, 'caused the evening to pass in the most enjoyable fashion'.

Jabez (a name he nowadays tried to avoid: though showing little resentment at the routine insults he took from the Tory *Express*, he did complain about them calling him Jabez) had won Burnley in February 1889, after three failed attempts – at Croydon, Walworth in south-east London and Doncaster – to regain his place in the Commons. He fought and lost Walworth in the general election of July 1886, a contest that arrived unexpectedly when a huge Liberal defection brought about Gladstone's defeat over Irish Home Rule. From an initial field of eleven Jabez secured the nomination, and pushing ahead of the favourite by making the better speech on Home Rule. He threw himself into the Walworth contest with his usual energy and enthusiasm, staging well-attended meetings around the constituency. No campaign in the district, said the *South London Press*, had created more excitement than this one. But the tide was flowing against the Liberal party and it swept the Conservative home in Walworth on 7 July with an increased majority.

Jabez's nomination as the Liberal candidate in Doncaster in February 1888 was achieved by a typical piece of opportunism. Jabez was no stranger to Doncaster. He had property there and at some stage had acquired the *Doncaster Gazette* and its printing works. The seat had been won at the 1885 election by a Croydon radical Liberal, Walter Shirley Shirley. He had kept it in the general election the following year, though with a sharply reduced majority. There had been rumours in the town through the winter that Shirley was thinking of leaving Parliament. Shirley denied them furiously. 'I have no intention of relinquishing my political career,' he declared, 'and shall probably remain member for Doncaster as long as the present parliament lasts.'

However, on 7 February Shirley wrote to constituency officers announcing that he was resigning. 'I feel it to be necessary, for the present at all events,' he told them, 'that I should give my undivided time and thought to the work of my profession [as a barrister].' The news had come to him as a complete surprise, Jabez told a meeting at Mexborough in the Doncaster constituency the following night. That claim hardly squared with the fact that he had already published his election address, and was now holding his first meeting.

A bruising contest ensued. The Liberal Unionist candidate – from that section of the Liberal party which had defected over Home Rule, and was now allied with the Conservatives – was the Hon. W. H. Wentworth-Fitzwilliam, a bit of a mouthful for an election poster, perhaps, but a local man, and a nob. 'Mr Fitzwilliam,' the Tory *Doncaster Chronicle* enthused, 'is not only a Yorkshireman, but a Yorkshire gentleman, with his whole time at disposal and with a zealous and very proper ambition to represent his own county, and that of his family for centuries past, in the House of Commons.' Jabez, by contrast, was 'the stranger now within these gates – the alien and wanderer who comes knocking at our door from Tamworth, where they rejected him, and from his own town of Croydon, where they would not have him'. What he wanted from Doncaster, alleged his assailants at the *Chronicle*, was a political base while he got on with what really interested him – promoting and running companies. Also, he was a separatist, happy, like his leader Gladstone, to see Ireland lost to kingdom and empire.

Jabez was indeed an outspoken Home Ruler now, claiming that he had believed in it longer even than Gladstone. But that did not make him a separatist. Separation, he said, would leave Ireland 'a melancholy island in the middle of the sea'. Nor, for that matter, was the Irish leader Parnell a separatist: Jabez would pay £25 to anyone who could prove that he was. Ireland was a consistent theme at his meetings, along with his devotion to the interests of the working class. Coldwells, that peripatetic endorser of Jabez's empathy with the working classes, was as always on hand to deliver this message.

Still, Doncaster rejected the interloper. On 23 February, Jabez was beaten by 211 votes – and this at a time when the tide elsewhere had been running for the Liberal party. It proved to be one of only two seats the party lost between the elections of 1886 and 1892. 'We have been defeated [cries of "bribery!"] by a small majority,' Jabez told his supporters after the count. 'We have polled on a bad register some hundreds of votes more than Mr Shirley polled in 1886. Personally, the result is a small matter, but I did wish that this division should send a word of comfort to Ireland at the present time.' Jabez's supporters also blamed their disappointing performance on their candidate's name. Electors must have mistaken him, it was claimed, for the Conservative chief secretary for Ireland, Arthur Balfour – a man, Jabez claimed with extraordinary chutzpah, who brought disrepute to the good name of Balfour.

But he made no mistake at Burnley. His capture of the Liberal nomination in this East Lancashire seat was uncannily similar to his arrival in Doncaster. Through the winter of 1888–9 concern had been brewing up in the Burnley press over the absences of their Liberal MP, Mr Slagg. He had voted only sixty-one times in the past two parliaments. He was missing big Burnley occasions – even the opening of the new town hall in October 1888 – sending his regrets and pleading a passing indisposition. People who had seen him declared that he looked poorly. By the beginning of February he felt he could not continue, and told his constituency party so on the 13th. But the first that anyone else knew of it came on the 21st. And who should arrive at Manchester Road station that afternoon, election address in hand, but J. Spencer Balfour.

He established his headquarters at the Thorn Hotel, met a deputation from the local Liberal council as soon as he'd had his tea, and won their warm approbation. Accepting their invitation to stand, he said that as a good soldier in a good cause he would obey the request as if it were an order. He did not think of his own convenience or interests. The writ for the by-election was moved the very next day.

The Tories and Liberal Unionists were fatally unready, so they blustered. Far from succumbing to local pleadings, they said, the candidate had been sprung on Burnley by the Liberal whips in London. He had no connections with Lancashire. He might promise the Liberals that his parliamentary role would come first, but in practice he would never be able to reconcile the representation of Burnley with his huge and demanding business interests at home and abroad – now expanded, the Directory of Directors for 1889 revealed, by the inclusion of a seat on the board of the Egyptian Lakes Reclamation Company. Jabez, it was generally recognized, was all about money: as one Burnley councillor put it, he was 'like a ratten terrier, he knew as soon as he geet his noas in a hoyle if there was ony brass in it'.

The Conservatives talked of finding a charismatic candidate to take Jabez on: Austen Chamberlain, John Albert Bright, H. O. Arnold Forster – all sons of Liberals who had broken with Gladstone over Home Rule. But while they hesitated, Jabez was already campaigning. He talked a lot about Ireland – 'a question as great and as holy as had ever inspired or thrilled the hearts of men' – as he probably would have done even if Burnley had not contained a growing population of families who had immigrated from Ireland. He pledged himself to the welfare of working-class people and, although he was known as a mine-owner, managed to win the endorsement of Burnley's miners. He declared his commitment to temperance while having a cordial meeting with the local licensed victuallers, expressing his deep sympathy with the difficulties of their trade. When nominations closed, he was the only candidate in the by-election. A grand reception was held, where with his wife's sister Mrs van Neck, her husband and Alderman Coldwells of Croydon beside him he was duly declared elected – just six days after he first set foot in the town.

Two years ago, he exulted in his victory address, Burnley had become the first town in England to show that the people of England were changing their views on Ireland. Now it was the first constituency to elect a Gladstonian candidate unopposed. Those words no doubt further inflamed the furious disputes in the local Conservative party about their failure even to put up a candidate. If they felt they had been stitched up, that was because they had been.

There were four Balfours in the Commons already, including his *bête noire* Arthur, the future Conservative leader. Jabez took to calling himself Balfive. In other ways, too, the House of Commons he entered as Member for Burnley had changed since his first incumbency. The 1884 Reform Act had broadened the male electorate – at Burnley the number entitled to vote was up from 7,000 to 10,000. The 1883 Corrupt and Illegal Practices Prevention Act had cleaned up elections by making votes harder to buy. That in turn made campaigns cheaper to run, and reduced the allure of candidates who came before local parties, as Jabez had done in Tamworth, accompanied by the sound of clanking money-bags. That did not, however, mean that the manipulative and the dodgy were swept away, as a string of parliamentary scandals during Jabez's second term at Westminster was shortly to demonstrate.

The first to go, in the month after Jabez arrived, was Colonel Hughes-Hallett, Conservative Member for Rochester. The official reason was ill-health; rheumatic fever had left him partly paralysed. But he would probably have had to have gone anyway. In 1887 he had come under sustained attack from the *Pall Mall Gazette* over his treatment of the daughter of the first husband of the colonel's deceased first wife. The colonel had at one point promised, it was alleged, to divorce his second wife and marry this young woman. Fed with information by the woman's solicitor, the *Gazette* claimed that the colonel had not only seduced her but taken £5,000 of her fortune of £40,000 (equivalent to over £2 million today), which he claimed he would use to purchase a property for her. In fact, he used it to pay his debts.

For a time his local party in Rochester stood by him, but the scandal stuck and in March 1889 he applied for the Chiltern Hundreds.* The affair had a bruising sequel. In April 1893 the colonel sued Mr Passmore Edwards, proprietor of *The Weekly Times and Echo*, and his manager and editor, Mr Kibblewhite, for libel after their newspaper reprinted the case against him in lurid terms. Passmore Edwards, a former MP for Salisbury, had stood as a Liberal against Hughes-Hallett at Rochester in the general election of 1883 and been beaten by him. But his motive in printing the allegations, he said, was the public interest. The *Times and Echo* had learned that the colonel, happily restored to good health, was planning to re-enter political life.

The libel trial was an odd affair. The judge, Sir Henry Hawkins, asked the colonel's solicitor at the outset whether

---

* Applying for the stewardship of the Chiltern Hundreds, an office of profit under the Crown, is the traditional device which enables MPs to disqualify themselves from membership of the Commons and so to resign.

there was really much point in going ahead with it. The young woman declined to give evidence, on the grounds that she was trying to forget the dreadful past and did not wish her name to be tarnished by being mentioned in the same breath as Hughes-Hallett's. To the surprise of the judge, Hughes-Hallett did not appear either. The colonel was determined to say nothing against the young woman, his counsel explained, and feared that if he went into the witness box he was bound to have questions put to him about the 'alleged seduction' and the birth of a child. Perhaps impressed by the judge's scepticism, the jury, having retired for a mere twenty-five minutes, found for the defendants, though adding that a reference to Sodom and Gomorrah in the newspaper's story was ill-advised.

Captain Edmund Hope Verney had seen service in the Crimea and the Indian Mutiny and came from one of the country's most celebrated families – one which had specialized in the parliamentary representation of Buckinghamshire long before he was first elected as Liberal MP for Buckingham in 1885. He had been deputy lieutenant for the county, deputy lieutenant for Anglesey and chairman of its quarter sessions, and a county councillor both in Anglesey and in London. None of this did him any good when in May 1891 he was convicted at the Central Criminal Court of conspiring to procure for an immoral purpose a girl of nineteen called Nellie Maude Baskett. That cost him his seat in the Commons, and he was expelled on 12 May, making him the first to endure this humiliation for thirty-four years (except for Charles Bradlaugh, whose crime had been refusing to swear the oath).

Two further expulsions followed the very next year. Edward Samuel Wesley de Cobain, MP for Belfast East, was the son of a Wesleyan minister and a prominent figure in the Orange Order. When a warrant was issued for his arrest on a charge of gross indecency with a man named Allan, he fled, first to Boulogne and then to the US. In March 1892 the Commons summoned him back to Westminster. When he failed to appear they expelled him. Just four days later, they turned out George Hastings, Liberal Unionist member for Worcestershire East, and a former chairman of Worcestershire County Council, deputy lord lieutenant and vice chairman of the quarter sessions, who had been convicted for a £20,000 fraud involving a will. When arrested he was found to be holding a visa for Turkey. In July 1893 the Irish Nationalist member for Mayo, John Deasy, applied for the Chiltern Hundreds after being convicted for an assault on his maid. 'The chosen of the electorate in Parliament and elsewhere have not been turning out particularly well lately' the *Morning Advertiser* sardonically observed after Deasy was fined £25, with costs.

Jabez's spell of nearly four years as MP for Burnley followed much the same pattern as his five and a half in Tamworth. He still spoke only rarely in the Commons, and asked few questions; when he did, they were usually linked to constituency issues, mostly involving working conditions in the mines and cotton mills. His voting record was moderate; his visits to the constituency were sporadic, but no more so than was the case with many MPs of the day. When he did come to Burnley, he tried to make a splash. On one occasion the train on which he was travelling from London missed its connection at Wakefield: rather than let down the meeting at which he was due to speak, he chartered a special train to arrive at the hall on time. That kind of gesture was expensive, but he could afford it, and it certainly helped get him talked about. Like Denry Machin in Arnold Bennett's novel *The Card*, he became identified 'with the great cause of cheering us all up'.

In London and Burnley Jabez constantly met deputations and usually sent them away feeling grateful for his attention. Working-class deputations – from miners, railway workers, weavers, millworkers – were especially cultivated, for already Labour candidates were running in local elections, and one was even adopted (though did not stand) for the 1892 election in Burnley's great rival Blackburn. Usually when Jabez came to town there were meetings to be addressed, many of which were not suitable for party politics, and here his speeches were astutely tailored to what his instincts told him his audience wanted to hear. Only the best butter would do. Burnley, he declared on at least one such occasion, was the most wonderful place in the world. Addressing the Salem Band of Hope Floral and Industrial exhibition, he delivered a paean of praise to the glories of nature, in Burnley especially, adding that in his youth he too had belonged to the Band of Hope. Prize-givings were a speciality, and to these he would usually bring a small entourage, often including his children James and Clara. Clara was now a widow. Her husband Walter Bishop had died of rheumatic fever at their home in June 1888, just six weeks after the birth of their son, also named Walter. Quite often another name would appear on the list of Jabez's attendants, that of a Miss Freeman – daughter of Henry Samuel Freeman, the saviour of Bembridge – who was always described as his ward, though was destined to become rather more than that. Now and then there were two Miss Freemans, both described as his wards.

Political occasions were more abrasive. Jabez was outspoken in championing Ireland even when speaking to audiences with no Irish connections. Whatever the doubts about Home Rule, he maintained, nothing could be less desirable than the status quo. He wanted to see the end of hereditary peerages. He believed that women should be given the vote on the same restricted basis as men. But as he liked to assure the licensed victuallers, one should not think worse of a man because he held different opinions, and even Conservatives mustered some grudging approval for Jabez's role in promoting the town and lifting its spirits. He got himself installed as the president of Burnley Football Club, on whose behalf he accepted the Lancashire Cup after their unexpected 2–0 defeat of Blackburn in 1890, telling his cheering audience that he saw no reason why they should not go on to claim the national Football Association cup at the Oval (where, characteristically he could not resist explaining, he served on the governing committee). He further announced, more controversially, that he planned to take the cup back to London to show it to his friends. He also addressed the Burnley Literary and Scientific Society on the subject of Dr Johnson, speaking for an hour and twenty minutes in praise of his hero, and quoting him at length –

appropriately in view of what would happen later – on 'The Vanity of Human Wishes'.

So despite opinions that some regarded as dangerously extreme, J. Spencer Balfour, MP, was a popular figure. When in March 1892 *Vanity Fair* did him the honour of printing a profile, complete with illustration by 'Spy' (the celebrated cartoonist Sir Leslie Ward) – a sign that a man had truly arrived – he ordered 13,000 copies, at a cost of £325, for distribution throughout the constituency. A history of the town published several years later and by no means biased towards the Liberal cause, said of him: 'Genial, openhanded, wealthy, the son of illustrious parents, thoroughly au fait with the art of winning popularity, he was the very beau ideal of a constituency representative. He was a born financier, who dealt with thousands as other men deal with sovereigns.' All of which helped to offset the doubts raised about the financial activities which had made him so open-handed and wealthy, now surfacing in the national press and duly relayed by the *Burnley Express* to J. Spencer Balfour's constituents.

In the summer of 1889 a substantial assailant attacked him. The *Financial Times* had been analysing a prospectus put out by the London, Edinburgh and Glasgow Assurance Company, of which J. Spencer Balfour, MP, was chairman, and was horrified by what it had found. Despite the sonorous words with which the company solicited further investment, the figures told a woeful story. Its gross assets totalled some £86,000; its liabilities ran to some £239,000. But the truth was even worse than the

overall figures revealed. Some of the assets were clearly ludicrously overvalued. The prospectus held out the bait of a juicy
new acquisition – 'a thoroughly sound, established and profitable business', which under their new arrangements should
pull in some £200,000 a year. In fact, the paper disclosed, this
profit-enhancing concern was the 'notorious' United Kingdom
Assurance Corporation ('and we congratulate the directors on
their circumspection in forgetting to mention its name'). The
principal skill of the LE&G, the paper asserted, had been in
cooking its books and inventing surpluses where only losses
existed.

The paper concluded: 'Our readers will, we are quite sure,
give the concern a wide berth, and will doubtless be on their
guard against any companies of which Mr Jabez Spencer
Balfour MP, of 4 Marlborough Gate, W, is a director. The shareholders of the companies from which this octopus draws
directoral fees will do well to see that their concerns are not
suffering from this same "management" or rather want of it,
which is so apparent in this company.' It went on to list the
enterprises – thirteen in all – on whose boards Jabez sat. As
ever, this list, taken from the Directory of Directors, underestimated the number of pies into which he had stuck his plump
finger.

As the LE&G's annual meeting was looming, Jabez would
be forced to reply. He did so apparently more in sorrow than
anger. It was perfectly right, he said, that the press should
examine in detail the financial performance of companies such
as his own, but in this case the *Financial Times* was making a

great fuss over nothing. Those who had attended these meetings before would know he had never shirked the fullest
disclosure of the detailed accounts. The figures, if correctly
interpreted, showed that the company could happily meet
every possible claim against it and still have funds left over. He
did not object to criticism, but here there was nothing to worry
about. Whether or not he was called an octopus did not
concern him in the slightest. His declarations were greeted
with cheers and cries of 'hear, hear'.

Confronted with this demonstration of shareholder complacency in the face of Jabez's masterful display of emollience, the
Financial Times returned to the fray. For downright audacity, it
wrote on 3 July 1889, his speech was absolutely unrivalled. The
'marvellous astuteness' with which the figures had been manip-
ulated disguised the essential truth that this company's finances
were even weaker than they had been a year before. As it
happened, there was at this time a court case brought against
five directors of the Yorkshire Provident Assurance Company,
all of whom lived in Burnley. A Commons committee had
demanded the company's prosecution for alleged malpractices.
The committee, the *Financial Times* charged on 17 July, had
picked the wrong target. Balfour's LE&G deserved its attention
much more than the Yorkshire Provident (whose directors,
when called to trial, would be cleared).

All of this was gleefully reported to Burnley by the *Express
and Advertiser*, which repeatedly challenged the town's MP to
answer the case against him. Jabez ignored all such calls. The
Financial Times moved on to other targets, and the *Burnley*

Express, lacking the expertise and resources to pursue these issues itself, let the matter drop.

In November *The Economist* joined the attack. This time the issue was a transaction engineered by the directors of two companies in which Jabez was prominent: the Assets Realization Company (ARC), of which he was chairman, and the Debenture Corporation, of which he was a director. As so often in Jabez's operations, the deal was easily done since the directors on either side were the same people. Shareholders of both organizations had been asked to agree that founders' shares of the Corporation, initially bought by them at £200 apiece, and then sold to the ARC for £150,000, should now be bought back by the Corporation for £300,000. But to make this work, very different stories had been told to the two groups of shareholders. Those of the ARC were being advised to part with the shares because the return on them was set to decline. Those of the Corporation were being assured that £300,00 was a very enticing price to buy at since the shares could be expected to sell in two years' time for twice that value. One side or other, *The Economist* pointed out, was being badly misled.

More generally *The Economist* was also concerned about the proliferation of directorships in the hands of certain MPs and peers. This was already a favourite theme of the *FT*'s rival, the *Financial News*, a paper created in 1884 and run by a buccaneering editor, Harry Marks, whose fearless and not always accurate assaults on companies that displeased him frequently landed him in the law courts. 'There are roughly two sorts of directors,' the *News* wrote in August 1888, 'the guinea pig and the successful businessman.' The guinea pig was the man who was on the board because his name looked good on the letter-head. Peers in particular, but also MPs and retired senior service officers, were constantly in demand for this purpose. Sometimes, Marks acknowledged, they took their duties seri-ously, mastered the affairs of the companies on whose boards they were serving, and became successful businessmen: yet running your own successful business made such demands on one's time that it must preclude effective service on boards of other companies.

'Every company which is desirous of obtaining government contracts is anxious to be represented in Parliament,' the *Financial News* declared in a later onslaught. 'And it is the custom to secure such representation by electing members of Parliament on boards of directors. In many, if not in most cases, they are so elected not for their business capacity, but solely for their parliamentary influence. They are paid large fees to repre-sent their companies in the House of Commons, to protect their interests when they are threatened, and to look after contracts when they are to be given out. In this way, the calling of parliamentary company directors has become a regular trade, and it is one that is not unremunerative. Men who, in their private capacities, would certainly not be considered desirable directors of companies, are deemed eligible as soon as they can add the magic letters MP to their names. A third-rate lawyer, a briefless barrister, the merest adventurer, once in the House of Commons, can count upon a safe income from this source.'

In July 1890 it printed a table exposing the biggest pluralists.

Twenty-six MPs held six or more directorships, with Jabez, who had fourteen, in second place behind the Conservative member for Stretford, J. W. Maclure, on sixteen. But even these figures underestimated the extent of his business involvements or his lust to acquire still more. In 1890, reports appeared that Jabez planned to acquire the radical London evening paper, the *Star*, whose founder, the Irish Nationalist MP for the Scotland division of Liverpool, T. P. O'Connor, had fallen out with his board. O'Connor was keen on the deal and was furious when it was blocked by one of his closest associates. Two years later, when the Balfour companies crashed, he was grateful for that intervention.

The Economist too had developed this theme in the previous month. 'It is notorious,' it said, 'that the average British investor is greatly attracted by a title, and it is much to be feared that some of our legislators have, frequently no doubt unwittingly, become "decoy ducks" at the bidding of unscrupulous company mongers... It is difficult to understand how a man can attend properly to the daily work which his constituents rightly expect of him, and at the same time direct the affairs of half a dozen or more companies carrying on, it may be, entirely different classes of business.'

Ideally, they would be told to give up either the business involvement or the parliamentary seat, though that, *The Economist* regretfully concluded, would perhaps be too much to ask. (It would still be too much to ask more than a century later. Figures published in 2003 showed that 179 MPs held directorships or had consultancy arrangements with companies

– a total greatly reduced since the 1980s by Labour's big majorities, since far fewer Labour Members than Conservatives figured in such arrangements. Just over a third of Conservative Members held directorships, against 9 per cent of Liberal Democrat MPs and 3 per cent of Labour's.)

Jabez was doubly vulnerable to this kind of attack. He was one of the most conspicuous pluralists, and additionally he had from the start made a point of attracting on to the boards of his companies just the kind of MP who was there for decoration rather than effect. But none of this seemed to disturb the voters of Burnley. The government of Lord Salisbury, installed in July 1886 for the seven-year term which was then the rule, was drifting towards its close. A general election was expected some time in 1892. Burnley's Liberal Unionists, backed by the town's Conservatives, had chosen as candidate a lawyer called Edwin Lawrence, who was neither a household name nor a local man, though, as his supporters repeatedly pointed out, he did have a wife who came from nearby Pendleton. Though quite late on he took a house on Todmorden Road in Burnley, his main addresses were Kensington Palace Gardens, London, and King's Ride, Ascot, which rather dented the claims of his supporters that he, rather than J. Spencer Balfour, was the natural choice for the working people of Burnley.

The dissolution of Parliament was announced for 28 June. At half-past six on the evening of Tuesday, 21 June, the sitting member for Burnley arrived at Manchester Road station to be greeted by a throng of supporters, who in their enthusiasm declined to use the appointed footbridge and raced across the tracks in front of the incoming train. The Briercliffe brass band was also in attendance and as Jabez stepped down from the train launched into a stirring rendition of 'Hail the Conquering Hero Comes'. Jabez was swept through the town to further applause, to which he responded by 'bowing to all and sundry, not forgetting the town hall officials mustered in force at the town hall windows'. He then addressed the crowd from the window of his habitual base, the Thorn Hotel (which was not, as his opponents liked to point out, a temperance institution).

The usual charges were thrown at him through the campaign, with his clutch of directorships perhaps rather more to the fore, but his enemies could not touch him. On Monday, 4 July, the voters of Burnley re-elected him by 6,450 votes to Edwin Lawrence's 5,035, giving him a majority of 1,415 votes (or 12.4 per cent), the most handsome seen in the town since the 1832 Reform Act.

With the Liberals back in power, the conquering hero hoped for office. The parliamentary sketchwriter Henry Lucy mocked him for his ambition. 'When . . . Mr Gladstone was forming his ministry,' he recalled after the crash, 'he received directly, or through the whips, some remarkable requests for preferment. Even with his long experience he was astonished at one or two cases where obscure members of the House of Commons, over-coming their natural modesty, put forth in detail claims to office. Among them was Mr Jabez Balfour, who confidently asserted his right to be appointed at least to an under-secre-taryship. Mr Balfour recalled how he had always been a liberal subscriber to the funds of the party; how he had fought two gallant battles under the Liberal flag at Croydon and Newington [Walworth]; how he had held Burnley for the true faith; how almost national in extent were his services outside politics in inculcating habits of thrift among the people through such institutions as, for example, the Liberator Society.'

That no job offer came was a serious blow to his pride; the party, he stormed, could expect no more money from him. But perhaps the Grand Old Man had been warned about Jabez, for his days at Westminster were numbered. On 28 August, just seven weeks after his triumph at Burnley, the portrait of Jabez which hung on the wall of the Croydon Liberal Club inexplicably crashed to the floor. Over the next eight days, his business empire, assembled with such assiduity, such *joie de vivre*, and – as the world would shortly find out – such an insouciant disregard for the law and for good business practice, did the same.

Part Two

8

The Skipper

'Tis done; the great transactions's done

Philip Doddridge (1702–51)

Jabez's empire collapsed because it was built on illusion. Honest companies at the end of each year worked out their assets and liabilities and their profits and losses and then decided, on the basis of their performance, how much they could afford to disburse in dividends and bonuses to their shareholders. Balfour accountancy worked the other way around. First, he and his colleagues decided what dividends and bonuses they needed to pay to keep a company looking healthy and profitable and encourage further investment; then the figures were cooked to fit. A further advantage of this system was that the better the figures, the greater the additional awards the directors could pocket. Throughout their history, the Balfour companies paid their directors handsome rewards for bringing in business which in the event simply augmented their losses. A century later, as scandals such as Enron and WorldCom broke, it would come to be called 'flattering the profits', though even that pretty expression underestimates the alchemy of manipulators like Jabez, who had no profits to flatter. One analysis after the crash found evidence of only one genuine profit in all the days of his operations – and that was no more than £2,500.

The so-called success of the project at Brading Harbour, for instance, so exuberantly celebrated ten years before at the Spithead Hotel, was pure fiction. The figures in the books represented an unequivocal triumph: acquired in 1876 for £39,000, the Brading site was said to be worth £359,000 ten years later, £461,000 in 1890 and around half a million when the Balfour Group collapsed. The sea defences were holding and Bembridge was looking prosperous. Yet the total receipts from the property over the years had been just over £11,000. The value of every conceivable asset, even the oysters deep in their oyster beds, had been inflated. Just as the locals predicted, the claims made for the project had been ludicrously optimistic. The loss to date was around £300,000.

Balfour accounting commanded an array of techniques for concocting profits. Jabez's companies revalued their assets, as for the Brading Harbour scheme, at well above what they were worth. They counted in money which was, at best, hoped for rather than realized, as if it were safely now in the bank. Sometimes the arithmetic was ingenious. Land at Meersbrook Park, Sheffield, had been bought for £577 an acre. Two of the most desirable bits were sold at £1,250 an acre; then all the remaining land was revalued at £1,250 an acre and the difference shown as a profit. Fictitious transactions were engineered between companies, inflating profits long enough to impress the shareholders and satisfy the accountants. Then further fictitious transactions took place to inflate the apparent profits of whichever company was next to report. Thus in September 1882 the Lands Allotment Company bought an estate at Ilford for £52,000; in the following January, it sold it on to the House and Lands Investment Trust for £60,000, inflating the LAC's paper profits; later in the same month the H&LIT sold it on to Hobbs and Co. for £74,000, boosting the takings of the H&LIT. That was what happened in theory: in practice no money changed hands.

Occasionally there were transactions between the companies in which no inflation occurred. That, Jabez's henchman George Brock would later explain, was simply to create the impression that something was happening. Above all, they helped themselves to the money that poor and thrifty people had invested in the Liberator Building Society, believing it was secure. As they raked through the wreckage after the crash, investigators found abundant traces of all of these malpractices.

Nothing in these manoeuvrings was riper than the story of Binfield Bird. The Lands Allotment Company had originally operated without a surveyor or valuer. It rectified this omission by appointing George Newman, who had been running his own business, George Newman and Co. But doubts arose over the accuracy of some of his valuations, and Jabez was persuaded, no doubt reluctantly, by one of his more worrisome colleagues that an independent valuation might be of use to the company. Accordingly he turned to a leading London estate agent, Driver and Co. The work was taken on by a senior partner, Robert Collier Driver, assisted by an employee called

Binfield Bird. Having examined a list of properties against Newman's valuations, the pair concluded that the doubters were right. Some – not all – of these properties were seriously overvalued; one, at Romford, was worth only half what Newman had said. So Driver prepared his report, only to be informed by Bird that the company no longer needed it. The directors had changed their minds. Driver accepted this decision, took his fees, and forgot the matter.

What he didn't know was that Bird, before joining Driver and Co., had worked for an Isle of Wight company and was well known to Jabez. The reason the directors no longer wanted his survey was that Bird had been hired to provide another, which duly reported that Newman had *under*valued the properties. Jabez congratulated Bird on his work, rewarded him (though not of course on the scale of the fees he had paid to Driver) and gave him a seat on the board.

Jabez's report to shareholders on the Binfield Bird episode catches him at his most self-righteous and shamelessly duplicitous. 'I have never lacked the courage of my opinion,' he told them, 'and if it had been necessary in this bad year for land companies generally, though not for us, to pay only 5 per cent or none at all, I should have had no scruple in coming down to this meeting and advocating that course... We naturally reverted in the first instance to our surveyor. Having had a great deal of business with him, I don't believe a more capable or straightforward or honest man exists. But this is a wicked world, and people are always willing to impute evil motives, and it might have been suggested he was not an independent man, so I proposed we should go as far as possible to the head of the profession. Of course, we might have gone to such firms as that of Sir J. Whittaker Ellis or Messrs Driver, but we could not have hoped for the same personal attention as we secured (Mr Bird).' That was too ripe even for Balfour's faithful henchman Brock. He deleted the denial of Driver's involvement from the final report; also, rather endearingly, the reference to the wickedness of the world.

As to fictitious transactions, directors of Jabez's Lands Allotment Company, contemplating some dubious deal with his House and Lands Investment Trust, were unlikely to balk at what they were asked to do, since the board of one heavily overlapped with the board of the other. Having, in their capacity as directors of the H&LIT, offered to buy some property at an inflated price from the LAC, they would then reconstitute themselves as the board of the LAC and gracefully accept the offer. The boards were not totally interchangeable, but they all came from Balfour's stable, and sometimes only two or three members were gathered together when deals of this kind were clinched. Indeed, on occasion, subordinates would later testify, Jabez would get them to add to the minutes the names of directors who were not actually there.

'As regards the relations of the various companies one to another,' Jabez assured one annual general meeting of the Liberator Building Society, 'I should like to say in the most distinct manner possible that each institution is entirely and absolutely independent of the others, and not in any way dependent on each other.' Nobody pointed out, though the facts were on the record, that no fewer than five of the society's directors served on the boards of other companies in the group. (The pattern is made plain by the table compiled for the *Westminster Gazette*'s post-crash analysis of the Balfour Group in the Appendix.) Directors of the London and General Bank were unlikely to challenge the loans which the bank made to Jabez's satellite companies since they were also part of the group that ran those companies; and in any case, the bank was under instruction always to honour the cheques of Balfour companies, however dire the state of the company's finances.

Nearly all the bank's business was done with Balfour companies. Yet its attitude to outsiders who wanted its money was surprisingly insouciant too. That was certainly the case when a financier called Kenyon Benham called on the bank in his capacity as secretary of a hospital in the West End. Benham, a man whose lavish lifestyle, with a fine address in Piccadilly and a county seat in Tunbridge Wells (where he generously offered to establish a town fire brigade, but never got round to paying for its uniforms), persuaded George Brock to advance him £49,000 on the security of a will. The will, needless to say, disappeared: someone, Benham explained, had left it on an underground train. Benham was sentenced after the crash to fourteen years' penal servitude for this and other offences, and despatched to Parkhurst prison, where Jabez himself was later to spend some time.

If the bank was in Jabez's pocket, so too were those experts who were supposed to be keeping an eye on his finances. Sometimes auditors asked awkward questions, but mostly they simply signed the accounts, out of either complacency or pure incomprehension. The auditors of the H&LIT at one stage were a retired non-conformist minister and Jabez's tailor in Wallingford.

Reprehensible in the company's early years, such practices became spectacularly undesirable when, after 1880, the Balfour Group left its allegedly philanthropic ambitions behind and moved into big league property. In the early days, the speculative builder had been seen as the enemy: as Jabez assured the Liberator's annual meeting in 1872, the words 'No speculative builders need apply' were written over its doors. It remained an unresolved question how much he had meant it then. Significantly, the building society had come into existence *after* the Lands Allotment Company, and there were those who believed it had always been Balfour's intention in setting up the Liberator to milk it for all it was worth. All but one of the LAC's directors sat on the board of the Liberator Building Society.

But certainly, the poor but thrifty non-conformist clientele for which the Liberator had ostensibly been created had little now to gain from the group's operations, which dealt almost exclusively in grand projects. Luxurious landmark hotels and apartments for the conspicuously well-to-do dominated the horizon. It was specifically for this grand design that the builder Hobbs and his company had been taken into the fold.

'Spencer Balfour's Palaces' the *Financial Times* called them when it sent its reporters on a tour of inspection after the crash. 'Whitehall Court', it reported, 'is a set of model dwellings on the Thames Embankment, adjoining the National Liberal Club, and admirably adapted for lodging the class of people who subscribe to such institutions as the Liberator Building Society. For an annual rental of £250 they can get a suite of six rooms, with the use of hydraulic lifts, and the services of a staff of servants, including gorgeous hall porters dressed like Lieutenant Dan Godfrey, of the Coldstream Guards band, in his full regimentals. There are marble halls with tiled floors, electric light throughout, and all the most modern improvements, such as are not known even in the similar buildings called Peabody Dwellings. The only drawback to which we can point is that the vacant suites at £250 per annum are dark and have a wretched outlook; but for £600 a year any member of the Liberator with sufficiently good references, can get a suite overlooking the river and beautifully light and airy. The only member of the Society who, so far as we know, has embraced the opportunity of living there is Mr Spencer Balfour.'

Even grander though, for any Liberator subscriber who fancied a smart London address, was Hyde Park Court, close to the Albert Gate, and still in existence today as an upmarket hotel, conveniently situated opposite Harvey Nichols department store. The illustrated brochure produced to market Hyde Park Court would have had English non-conformity licking its lips. 'The splendid erection, known as Hyde Park Court, situated in the main thoroughfare of Knightsbridge, overlooking in the rear Rotten Row, with the Park and Serpentine beyond, and fitted with every modern improvement is, of its kind, unrivalled. It is built of red brick with stone dressings and

ornamentation and the numerous balconies and balustrades of
stone and iron, the double ascent of bays, the portico supported
on massive columns, and the railed turret poised upon the
extreme top, combine to give it an appearance of grace,
elegance and solidity...Apartments in this palace cost only
£500 a year, which includes the benefit of the culinary department, presided over by Monsieur Alexandre Lacamp, and the
services of a large staff, including – at present – a valet to nearly
every occupant, and the use of "an almost endless succession of
lavatories."'

But how sad it seemed now. 'The valets are idle, the electric
light shines in vain, the billiard rooms are empty, even the
endless succession of lavatories fails to charm, and the concern
is in liquidation.' And what had it cost, all this extravagance?
The National Liberal Club was known to have cost a quarter of
a million or so and the even grander Whitehall Court, now
tacked on to it had probably taken three times that sum.
Helpful people at Hyde Park Court had told the *Financial Times*
that it must have cost at least half a million. The paper
assumed that the money had come straight from the Liberator.
'There could surely be no more complete prostitution of the
privileges afforded by the [Building Societies] Act than to use
money, provided as a rule by poor people, for the purpose of
making advances to speculative builders who employ it in
erecting tenement palaces so gorgeous that few people can be
found wealthy enough and luxurious enough to rent them.'

This catalogue excluded perhaps the most ambitious project
of all, as yet far from completed: a mighty hotel on the north

bank of the Thames, just off the Strand, on a three and a quarter acre site bought from the Cecil family, whose head was the Marquess of Salisbury. This was designed to become the biggest hotel in Europe, far ahead of any other in London for its comfort and glamour, with a thousand rooms, a magnificent banqueting hall, and a range of attractions especially designed to tempt American visitors. So ambitious were Jabez's plans that some called it 'Balfour's folly'. It was still far from complete when the Balfour companies crashed in 1892, but the official receiver persuaded shareholders to put up additional funds, and in 1896 it opened as the Hotel Cecil. It was swept away in 1928, when its contents were disposed of in one of the longest such sales of the twentieth century, realising some £1.6m. In its place rose an unendearing successor, Shell-Mex House.

Fat dividends every year and bonuses to go with them, and rich pickings for directors who could also pick up fat commissions – it was all very sweet while it lasted. As Edmund J. Cleary wrote in his account of Balfour in the *Dictionary of Business Biography*, so long as the Liberator continued to grow apace, the precise nature of Jabez's enterprise could remain hidden. But by now he and his confederates had seriously overreached themselves, and had done so just at the moment when the British economy was running into recession. Part of the problem was investment in another of Jabez's subsequent destinations, Argentina. It was over-confident investment there which in November 1890 helped bring the great city house of Barings into a near-terminal crisis, with liabilities topping £21m. With a mixture of cajoling and bullying, mostly in the

City of London, where many companies had reason to fear the collapse of Barings would bring them down too, the governor of the Bank of England William Lidderdale engineered a rescue operation which averted that disaster.

None of this, Jabez assured his shareholders, was any menace to them. 'I always claim for this Trust,' he told the annual meeting of the H&LIT in March 1892, 'that we are independent of the fluctuations and vicissitudes of the Stock Exchange ... We hear from time to time that the Stock Exchange and markets generally will not improve until certain things happen to Messrs Murietta and Messrs Baring and in regard to the state of trade in the Argentine Republic. But I am glad to think we do not depend on the state of trade in the Argentine Republic.'

In fact, as he knew all too well, funds had been getting seriously scarce in the Balfour Group. The increasingly excessive rates at which the Balfour companies were now borrowing were one indication of that. By 1891, and even more in the early months of the following year, there were unmistakable signs of impending crisis as Hobbs and Co. ran up runaway debts, and the rest of the group did what they could to save it; for if Hobbs and Co. crashed, the London and General Bank would be in deep trouble and the rest of Jabez's empire with it. Not that Jabez gave even the mildest hint of such things when he spoke to the bank's AGM in February 1892. On the contrary, he talked rather wistfully of the need for the bank to grow greater. His dream was still that of the biblical Jabez: the enlargement of coasts. As long as they remained in their present position, he said, they were bound to be regarded as a mere building society bank, servicing the Liberator, the H&LIT, the LAC, and 'other respectable institutions of a similar character'. He appealed to shareholders to try to build up the business, emphasizing the view of an 'eminent authority' in the City of London that all was going well for the enterprise. He omitted to add that he had recently sold much of his personal holding.

Things had nearly come badly unstuck when the auditors examined the state of the bank in the spring of 1891. William Theobald, brother of Jabez's henchman Morell, wrote a stiff report, declaring what by then was undeniable: that the assets claimed by the bank were simply not justifiable. The auditors further insisted that no dividend ought to be paid in the bank's present circumstances. Unless Jabez and Brock could find some way around it, they were faced with having these unpalatable and confidence-threatening truths emerge at the next general meeting. But these old hands knew from experience how to deal with a challenge like that. The tactic was to pretend that it hadn't happened. They had, after all, faced similar challenges over the years, and brushed them aside. Once before, the Theobald brothers had abandoned their posts as auditors. In November 1887 there had been worries enough at a meeting of the LAC board for Balfour, Dibley and Brock to be asked to draw up a financial report on the state of the company. That decision, however, was struck out of the minutes the next time the board met because it was clear the report could reveal only one thing: that the LAC was insolvent.

Even the normally tractable George Dibley had resigned his

directorship of the Lands Allotment Company in 1889 after a dispute with Jabez over the endorsement of bills, and in protest against Jabez's insistence on making the company acquire shares in another of his queasy ventures, the Electric Construction Corporation. He felt wounded, too, because Jabez had charged him with being disloyal by selling some of his shares. Even Hobbs and the solicitor Wright, the architects of the group's coming misfortunes, had walked out on Jabez at some time or other, only to return out of loyalty to the man they called 'the skipper'.

The most serious challenge, though, had come from within the skipper's own family. Leonard Balfour Burns was the product of the union of Jabez's sister Cecil with the Revd Dawson Burns. Jabez, Leonard would later say, had been his friend and protector from the age of fifteen, had hired him at twenty-one in 1875 to be secretary of the H&LIT, and had promoted him in 1886 to a place on the board. But as he grew older and more confident, Leonard could no longer acquiesce in practices he had been worrying over for some time. In 1890 he wrote Jabez a letter explaining that he had for a while been seriously considering his position as a director, and had now decided that he ought to resign. 'I feel it quite impossible to concur any longer in the policy of increasing the capital amounts of the large properties by charges in respect of interest. This has been done year after year until these accounts in many cases are swollen to figures which in my opinion are now far beyond the value they can ever possibly realize.'

These problems were all the more serious, Leonard wrote,

because of the absence of professional auditors. He believed the directors ought to be given the protection of a periodical professional valuation of their assets. Additionally he was worried that when so many large transactions were taking place between the Trust and the Liberator, a majority of the Liberator board were also directors of the Trust. He concluded: 'I am taking this step now rather than at the end of the current year, because, feeling as I do that I could under no circumstances be a party to the issue of another balance-sheet based on the same principle as hitherto, I might by raising these objections at a late hour cause embarrassment. Nothing is further from my wish than to do this; on the contrary, I wish, having regard to what I feel to be my duty in this matter, to occasion as little trouble and friction by my retirement as possible. Trusting you will bring this matter before your Board on Monday, I am – Leonard Balfour Burns.'

Too trusting, as it turned out. At one of the subsequent cases arising out of the crash, the secretary of the H&LIT testified that though Jabez had flourished the letter in front of the board, he had never actually read it to them. Whether or not that was true, Leonard's old colleagues seemed untroubled by his departure. George Brock wrote him a chilly letter, regretting his departure and expressing surprise that he'd now raised these objections when he had never done so before.

When faced with dissident auditors in the very next year, 1891, Jabez withheld their damning report. Instead, he promised them that he would warn shareholders at the annual general meeting of what it contained. But he did so in a manner which concealed much more than it revealed and left the shareholders unaware of the bank's situation. Nor did he disclose their warning against declaring a dividend: instead he announced his standard 7 per cent. The tactic was repeated the following year when Morell Theobald, who was far more deeply involved in Jabez's operations than his brother William, belatedly tried to save himself. In April 1892 he despatched a letter to Brock resigning his directorship. After more than thirteen years on the board of the LAC, having felt some anxiety, and having reviewed the accounting policy laid down by Balfour, he thought the time had come for the facts to be faced: estates at Romford and Tilbury, which like so many others had been entered in the books at well above what they were worth, should be put at their proper value, and the whole policy should be reviewed. His colleagues dealt with these valid objections in their now traditional manner – they ignored them. Theobald's resignation was not reported at the annual meeting. Those who perceptively asked where he was were told he had left on grounds of ill-health.

But prevarication could not work for ever, and by the autumn of 1892 Jabez's empire was well beyond saving. The fact that they now had to offer interest at 17 or even occasionally 20 per cent to bring in the funds they so desperately needed was one proof of that. The immediate problem was the now insuperable debt run up by the builder, cricket promoter, organizer of cultural evenings and twice mayor of Croydon, James William Hobbs. The state of his organization made the rest of the group look efficient and honest by comparison.

Apart from his debts in his public capacity, Hobbs was in debt to the group solicitor H. Granville Wright, who, contrary to the rules of the Law Society, was threatening Hobbs with what he would do if he did not soon get his money.

According to testimony at their subsequent trial, it was Wright who came up with a solution. Hobbs should, in effect, find the money he needed to pay off his debt by stealing it from the Liberator. The plot had also involved Hobbs's clerk, George Kentish, 'a hard, commonplace little man', whose sister was married to Hobbs. Kentish was also a product of Croydon non-conformity, a deeply religious man, according to friends, lecturer to the Band of Hope and secretary of the Croydon Temperance union. However, he was also in debt, not least because of an action brought by a publication called *The Ironmonger* against him in his capacity as sole proprietor of the West Central Engineering Company.

Hobbs found some of the money by inventing bills he claimed to have paid – to his cousin's wife for instance, though when asked she denied any such dealings. He and Kentish also inflated the wages bill by £30 or £40 a week. Kentish then took £5 a time while Hobbs took the rest. The judge at Hobbs's trial, Sir Henry Hawkins, a man sometimes known for his severity as Hanging Hawkins, summed it up succinctly: 'Hobbs robbed the company and you robbed him.'

So Hobbs and Co. went under, with consequences which Jabez must have foreseen. The ruined enterprise owed more than £2m to the London and General Bank, none of which was recoverable. Thus the Bank was doomed too. None of the other companies in the Balfour Group could help, since they were all hopelessly debt-ridden. Not one – not even the jewel in Jabez's crown, the Liberator Building Society – had any chance of survival.

On 1 September 1892, cheques were returned unpaid. On 2 September, the doors of the bank were found to be bolted. 'Temporary suspension of business' said a notice pinned to the door. Enquiries were referred to the City solicitors Bonner Wright and Thompson, in which H. Granville Wright was a partner, but those who called there for advice were repulsed. The firm, they were told, had severed all connections with the Balfour Group three months earlier. Some of the people who came to the doors were deeply distressed, the bank's caretaker told reporters. One man, who had recently paid in £700 was 'nearly mad with excitement and grief'. The plight of a woman who turned up with two little children only to find the doors locked against her had been particularly painful to witness. Another man told reporters that he had dreamed in the previous week that the bank would crash, and had recounted this dream to his friends. Yet in spite of that he had paid in a further £100 the very next day. Now he seemed to have lost the lot.

As the bank locked its doors against a clamorous public, there still seemed a chance that something might be saved. The *Financial Times* did no more than express concern that the Liberator's resources might fall short of meeting the bank's obligations. Even the *Burnley Express*, always eager to revel in the discomfiture of the borough's MP, assured its readers that the crisis was less than terminal.

Jabez himself was calm and constructive. True, he was eager to minimize his involvement, telling a Burnley interviewer that over the past eight years he had virtually ended any direct connection with the society, having moved onto other things. Yes, he was listed as vice-president on the letterhead, but that was a purely honorary position. The predicament of the companies, he explained, was the fault of other ill-managed building societies whose recent collapse had punctured investors' confidence. As for the failure of Hobbs and Co., that was hardly the disaster some claimed. It was well known, he said, that the society had recently been investing in major projects, and obviously big schemes in the heart of London were more vulnerable than smaller schemes in the suburbs. Had these projects only been brought to completion, the talk now would have been about spectacular profits, not losses.

All was not lost. There was hope of a reconstruction, he told an extraordinary meeting of the House and Lands Investment Trust on 24 October. If half a million of debentures could be raised, the trust's assets would become realizable within twelve months and the losses involved would be greatly minimized. The Offical Receiver, C. J. Stewart, saw little hope of that. The situation he was now uncovering, he told a meeting of creditors and shareholders of the Liberator on 31 October, was 'the most disgraceful that has ever been heard of'. There might be talk of reconstruction, but the real question was whether anything was left to reconstruct.

That was typical, Jabez argued, of the negative spirit in which the problem was being approached. He intended to set to work on a reconstruction, even if that meant abandoning other interests, his parliamentary career included – though it was not until November that he sought to resign his seat by applying for the Chiltern Hundreds. Others were less optimistic. On 19 September, William Blewitt, of Blewitt and Tyler, solicitors, a director of the London and General Bank, failed to return to his home at Wanstead in Essex at the end of a day in the City. Two youths discovered him lying in Epping Forest, his throat gashed and his wrists cut. He was able to speak a few words – enough to make clear he had been intent on suicide – one of them recognizable as 'trouble'. Dr Bodilly hurried over from Woodford, stitched up the wounds and got Blewitt to Dalston hospital. He survived.

The collapse of the London and General imperilled other banks, the Birkbeck especially. The most panicky scenes in the City for years were reported as clients besieged its offices. One of the last to leave the scene was robbed of £1,100 by a pickpocket; others, too, having extracted their money, were relieved of £100 or more by unfeeling assailants.

The deeper the Official Receiver dug into the Balfour Group's ramshackle finances, the more alarmed he became. The impression conveyed at the annual meeting of the Liberator Building Society seven months before the crash that all was well and business was expanding had been, 'to use a mild term, absolutely misleading'; business had in fact been falling away. The total indebtedness of the Society was thought to be over £3m. Its reserve fund, which its directors claimed stood at around £90,000, had only £10,000 in it. The bank, now in liquidation, had debts of £80,000 and appeared to have no assets at all.

There were loans recorded as assets, but these loans were to Balfour companies, which could never repay them. Alongside Hobbs's debts of £2m, the Real Estates Company owed £481,000 and though he put no figure on the plight of the H&LIT that too faced liquidation. As for the oldest constituent of the group, the Lands Allotment Company was owed half a million by Newman and Co. alone. 'Loud angry cries for Balfour' rang through the Holborn Restaurant at the 31 October meeting, but Jabez was missing. George Brock, a solicitor called Booth who served on the board, and Jabez's son James, who was twenty-four, all tried to speak, but what they said was howled down. Those who faced ruin, as many did in that hall, knew who to blame.

On 4 November, Jabez reappeared at an extraordinary meeting of the Lands Allotment Company. The mood on the platform was optimistic: if £100,000 could be raised in debentures, it was claimed, it would put the company beyond the power of anybody to jeopardize its future. One of the architects of this proposal, a man called Evans, warned shareholders not to antagonize Jabez, since they needed his goodwill and assistance to make the reconstruction work. Many present were unimpressed. 'Amid much noise and interruption', the Revd H. Jefford moved a resolution: 'that, in the estimation of honest men, Mr Spencer Balfour MP is no longer a fit and proper person [hisses, and loud cries of 'Order'] to represent any constituency in Parliament, and that he be requested to resign his seat.' The chairman (George Brock) ruled the motion out of order.

The mood was even more hostile when ' a large and excited meeting' of creditors and shareholders of the H&LIT assembled on 1 December to give Jabez what one reporter suggested was the worst quarter of an hour of his life. The Official Receiver was in the chair, and what he had to report was even gloomier than before. He had now examined in detail twelve of the Trust's properties, and there was not the slightest hope of any of them being sold for anywhere near its book value. Its reserve fund, claimed to be £36,000, had nothing in it at all.

There were noisy demands from the meeting for any directors present to identify themselves. Balfour, whose appearance was greeted with 'a hurricane of hisses', Pattison, Brock, Coldwells and another Croydon acolyte, F.R. Rocke were all there. Asked to reply to Stewart's indictment, Jabez said he would very much like to do so, but unhappily he did not have all the information he needed to hand. He should have been warned beforehand of the chairman's intended attack on him. 'I will pledge my word of honour,' he said (derisive laughter), 'that I did not know these specific points were going to be made.' He had been put in a very awkward position.

Despite what the chairman had said, the fact that the Trust had been intertwined with Hobbs and Co. had been very well known. Jabez greatly resented an allegation from the floor that the auditors had been 'playing his game'. He thought the chairman ought to protect him from such grossly discourteous language. 'I think, Mr Balfour,' said Stewart, 'you rather provoked the remark.' That was typical, Jabez stormed, of the unfair treatment to which he was being subjected. He felt keenly the disaster that had occurred. The whole current of his life had been changed by it. 'The gathering,' wrote one reporter, 'did not seem to appreciate the intensity of Mr Balfour's sorrow, and groaned and hissed at him again with great fervour.'

Subsequent meetings called by Stewart to pass on further appalling news to Jabez's victims were if anything even stormier. James Balfour, again attempting to speak on 20 December, was again dismissed as irrelevant. Cries of 'where's your father?' greeted poor James as he came forward.

The noise now grew so great that James gave up trying to reply and spoke to the chairman, who said: ' Mr Balfour says that to the best of his knowledge Mr Spencer Balfour is in Oxfordshire.'

There was no sign of Jabez in Burcot, however, and none in Whitehall Court either. Finding that Jabez was £10,000 in debt to his ruined bank, the Official Receiver sent staff to search his apartment in Whitehall Court, where they found very little apart from a piano, some paintings and some furniture, total value £200. Further enquiries, inconclusive since some of the books were missing, established the overall debts of the Balfour Group at more than £7m – the equivalent of something like £450m in the opening year of the twenty-first century. Samuel Wheeler, who had now taken over Stewart's inquiry, thought the most that he could recoup would be £27,000, of which only £11,000 had been recovered so far.

A further noisy meeting at the end of the month was treated to figures establishing just how wild the claims to company assets had been. The value of Whitehall Court had been claimed at £615,000; its actual value was £250,000. Brading Harbour's claimed value had been put at £500,000; its actual value was below £100,000. And so it continued. Again there were shouts for the guilty directors: this time it was Brock and his fellow Croydonian, Frederick Rocke, board member of three Balfour companies, who shamefacedly came forward to acknowledge them.

Jabez – the Great Liberator himself – was safe, at least for a while and perhaps, as he thought, for good, from the wrath of those he had ruined and from those whose work it would be to bring him to justice. He was putting 7,000 miles between himself and those who wanted retribution as he headed for a refuge on the other side of the world.

9

Señor Samuel Butler

O refresh us
Travelling through this wilderness

John Fawcett (1740–1818)

The Grand Hotel, Broadstairs, on its cliff overlooking the channel, was reputed to be the best in the town. Built ten years before, in 1882, at a cost of £78,000, the Grand, with its 100 bedrooms, its capacious reading and smoking rooms, its billiards hall, and its fine views over the sea towards Belgium, belonged, in its aspirations at least, to that class of lavish palaces built by Hobbs for Jabez's empire. Guests would be met at Broadstairs station by horse-drawn omnibuses supplied by the hotel management. Once installed, they could stroll along the cliff walk, past the little bandstand where a military band would often be playing, through the gardens opened by Princess Louise only that year and down to the picturesque harbour. The Grand is a block of apartments now, with a pub in the basement, but it still has a sense of the confidence with which it opened its doors to welcome the privileged and prosperous to the coast of Kent.

Here, on Sunday, 11 December 1892, a man presented

himself at reception to ask if a Mr Granville Wright was staying at the hotel. He was, though quite why is not clear. Was he perhaps enjoying a quiet weekend with his mistress, Mrs Maybury? Or could he have made it his base while he contemplated flight to safety across the Channel? If so, he was not going to make it, for Inspector Moore of Scotland Yard had been having him watched for some days. Mr Wright was summoned from his room and moments later was being escorted away to the station for the London train. It would all have been done most discreetly, with the reputation of the Grand not for one moment imperilled.

Mr Hobbs, the progressive builder, was not so fortunate. He had been holding one of the musical evenings of which he was famously fond and which Jabez loved to tease him about. Now the civilized tranquillity of the evening was interrupted by a knock on the door and an urgent summons. Inspector Moore, accompanied by Inspector Tunbridge, was anxious to have a word. The music was summarily halted, and the guests from whom he was taken said Hobbs had been deeply upset and had left loudly protesting his innocence.

Soon the news was all over Croydon. Wright's arrest was a matter of minor significance – 'a thin, weazened, and very irascible man' the *Croydon Times* called him, who was nowadays rarely seen in the town. But Hobbs...! Like Jabez, he had twice been mayor of the borough; his fame as a builder and entrepreneur had spread well beyond Croydon; his cricket ground, close to his splendid house at Norbury, had seen W. G. Grace himself in action, and one of Queen Victoria's sons, not to mention Murdoch's Australians. He was a cut above the irascible Wright and his arrest and appearance in court next day were enough to persuade the Croydon papers to rush out special editions. Each man was accused of forging a bill of exchange: Hobbs was additionally charged with stealing £29 from the Liberator Building Society. But more serious allegations were expected to follow.

News of the arrests was brought to Jabez at Burcot on 12 December. He left early next morning for London. It was not, he would later maintain, his intention then to flee impending prosecution. But flight, his City friends told him, was the only sensible course: his chances of getting a fair trial after all the angry meetings and vituperative press attacks were too thin to be worth considering and he would certainly face prison. He stayed overnight at Burcot on the night of 15 December. Local legend says that as the police came up one end of Jabez's drive, he made his escape from the other.

'I have never regretted any incident of my business life more than that unnecessary and damning flight,' he wrote in *My Prison Life*. 'It was no secret at the time that I went against my own wish, and that I acted upon what I believed was the best legal opinion in England.' But he had months of terrible strain and agitation, of unremitting and unsuccessful labour, of a kind few men would have survived: he was broken in mind and body.

Soon lurid rumours were circulating in the City about where he had gone. Sightings were confidently reported from Chile, Brazil and Spain. 'A well known barrister' told a London newspaper that he had bumped into Jabez somewhere in southern Europe. There were even, as one concerned Conservative complained to *The Times*, suggestions that it wasn't J. Spencer Balfour who had disappeared, but Arthur Balfour, the Marquess of Salisbury's nephew, lieutenant and later successor as Conservative leader.

In fact, on the morning of Sunday, 18 December, he caught the 11 o'clock train out of London for Dover, took a boat for Calais, and went on by train to Basle and then to Genoa; and there he embarked by steamer for Buenos Aires.

Argentina was a logical destination. It was 7,000 miles away from his creditors and although an extradition treaty had been negotiated three years before, it had never been ratified by the Argentine Parliament and so had no force. And even if the treaty were to be ratified, Jabez believed, no doubt on the basis of the 'best legal opinion' he had been given in London, that he would be safe, having arrived in Argentina before ratification took place. The British had been trying since 1890 to extradite a Mr James Coupe from Argentina, and had made no progress at all. Later, a Dr and Mrs Freeman had arrived in the country from Spain. Dr Freeman was wanted in London for assisting in causing the death of a woman called Ellen Franklin in the course of an illegal operation. Yet he remained safely in the Argentine capital, practising under the ingenious sobriquet Dr Manfree.

Though passenger lists for boats leaving Europe contained no trace of the fugitive, the government in London became increasingly sure that their man was in Buenos Aires. Certainty came at the end of February, when Mr Cuffe of the Treasury Solicitor's Office confirmed to the Home Office, on the basis of a report from Inspector Tunbridge, that four cheques from a Croydon bank had been changed in the city by somebody calling himself Samuel Butler. No doubt there was speculation the length of Whitehall as to why their quarry had adopted the name of the author of *Erewhon*. The real Samuel Butler had not yet published his more appropriate title, *The Way of All Flesh*.

The Home Office immediately prodded the Foreign Office, who in turn prodded Francis Pakenham, the British minister plenipotentiary in Buenos Aires, to put pressure on the Argentine government to get the treaty ratified. Unlike Jabez, Whitehall seemed confident that the treaty would work retrospectively, enabling Britain to get its hands on the villain of the Liberator affair as well, no doubt, as on Coupe and Freeman. But each time the message came back: there can be no extradition before ratification unless Britain agrees to 'reciprocity' – in other words that Argentina would have the right to demand extradition from Britain too, even without a treaty. And as Buenos Aires knew, there was never the slightest prospect of London agreeing to that.

Soon the language grew tougher. 'It is evident', wrote Home Office under-secretary Edward Leigh Pemberton to his counterpart in the Foreign Office, 'that it is now generally known that extradition cannot be obtained from that country, which is therefore becoming a refuge for English criminals of every class.' But Argentina remained unmoved.

George E. Welby, chargé d'affaires, had met the Argentine foreign minister, one of the minister's chief subordinates, and the procurator-general for the republic, and had reminded the foreign minister that this was the third serious case in which 'criminals' from England were not being handed over for trial. Yet the Argentine government was unready to take any serious steps to persuade the Congress to process some twenty-nine treaties now waiting for ratification. Then, in a passage of a letter to Lord Rosebery which some more cautious hand later crossed out but happily failed to eradicate, Welby wrote: 'I must further state to your lordship that it is extremely difficult to induce the deputies, who are for the most part a most worthless and venal body and who are responsible for many of the financial burdens with which this country is now loaded, to take any trouble or interest in any measure in which no pecuniary profits are to be derived, however beneficial they may be to the Nation. There are at present about seven extradition treaties awaiting the sanction of Congress, viz: Belgium, Switzerland, Russia, Italy and Germany...The greater number of Argentine deputies are men who have never left their own country and are little accustomed to modern usages or requirements and being of an arrogant and narrow-minded disposition they consider that their own constitution is all that is necessary and are therefore unwilling to accede to any changes which might be required in view of their present increasing intercourse with other Nations.'

By late March 1893, the whole world knew – for the case was being assiduously followed in Australia and the Americas as

well as in Britain – that the fugitive was living in a suburb of
Buenos Aires. Reports had also begun to appear of two young
women who had come out from England to join him, neither of
whom was his wife. They travelled under the pseudonyms of
Miss Baker and Miss Ferguson and when accosted by pushy
pressmen would merely blushingly say: 'We know nothing.'
The newspapers got as far as discovering that the girls were
Jabez's wards, the daughters of a business associate who had
died. Their true names, though, somehow still eluded them.
One young lady was now presenting herself in Argentina as
Mrs Butler, while the other described herself as Butler's sister-
in-law. In fact they were Ethel Sophia and Lucy Mary, the
eldest of the five daughters of Henry Freeman, the saviour of
the Brading Harbour project, who had died ten years earlier.

The legation in Buenos Aires, like newspaper readers in
Britain, were fascinated by this picture of the pretty young
mistress and the portly, waddling, fifty-year-old absconder.
Unfortunately every surviving official record fails to establish
which of the daughters was his mistress and which was his
spurious 'sister-in-law'. When they sailed back from Buenos
Aires in February 1894 press reports gave their names as
Miss L., or in one case Miss L. M., Baker and Miss E. S.
Ferguson. Lucy Mary's name appears on documents signed by
Jabez in his last days in London, so one might have assumed she
was the closer to him. But pointers to Ethel, the elder sister are
more persuasive. Victorian etiquette reserved the simple title
'Miss' for the eldest daughter, using Christian names for her
younger sisters. The name on the cheque that Jabez cashed in

Buenos Aires, thus giving away his whereabouts, was Ethel's. And press reports say that it was 'Miss E. S. Ferguson' who returned to Buenos Aires to resume her life with Jabez, which might seem to settle the matter – except that the passenger lists from the voyage show a Miss Baker, with no initial.

The safer conclusion would seem to be that Ethel Sophia was Jabez's mistress and Lucy had gone along on her initial visit to support her. But none of this is watertight, and the one piece of evidence which might have resolved all doubts – the passenger list of the ship on which Miss Freeman made her last voyage from Buenos Aires, when she used her own name – is untraceable. I must therefore give her the designation her contemporaries did: 'Miss Freeman'.

Once Jabez's presence in Buenos Aires became well known to British and Argentine authorities and to the press, the place became too hot for him, and he fled again: this time to Salta, a provincial town close to the border with Chile and 800 miles from the capital. The rail journey took fifty-six hours, and led to the first of Jabez's adventures on Argentine trains. His diary for 17 May 1893 records: 'Soon after dark, our train met with a serious accident, the engine, tender and luggage van being thrown off the line and smashed to pieces...Fortunately no lives were lost, the escape of the driver and stoker, who were pitched from their engine, being almost miraculous...It was a weird spectacle. The engine was lying on its side some yards from the line, and was belching out smoke and steam; the tender was standing on one end some little distance off, the first van was smashed to pieces, and the second was greatly damaged, and had turned almost across the line. A bullock, the cause of the mischief, was lying dead and bleeding and partially disembowelled under the wheels of the first passenger carriage.'

Jabez had difficulty extricating himself from the wreckage, but he and his 'lady friend' struggled out and waited around for eight hours before their journey continued. Fortunately, he recorded, they had just dined on the train and had biscuits and whisky with them. 'Accidents of this kind', he reflected, 'and from the same cause, are very frequent in this country, where great herds of cattle roam about, and where broken down fences and open gates abound.' The ubiquity of wandering cows formed part of his general complaint about the country that had given him refuge. From the conduct of their politics to the mending of the broken windows which were everywhere on display, Argentinians could or would not do things properly.

During his stay in Salta, Jabez kept a regular diary, sending extracts back to 'friends' in England, and certainly to his son. Some of these were later reprinted in the *Pall Mall Gazette*, under the title: 'The Diary of the Fugitive'. The circumstances that had brought him to Salta were left unmentioned.

These were turbulent times in Argentina. In the 1880s, a centralizing president, Julio A. Roca, had sought to stamp the authority of the capital on the provinces, establishing a new federal system and introducing a common currency. Initially these reforms brought years of relative calm and stability, but by 1890 the country had entered a phase of political and economic turbulence, with its provinces increasingly unwilling to recognize the authority of the central government. In that year, the collapse which so nearly brought down the great London house of Barings took the country into deep recession. 'We have been living in constant expectation of a revolution here,' Jabez noted in July 1894. 'There has been quite an epidemic of revolutions throughout the country.'

Jabez was not impressed by the way the central government attempted to quell revolt. Why, for instance, did they seek to boost the size of their fighting forces by press-ganging unwilling recruits, some of whom were certain to take the first opportunity to defect to the other side? The Republic, he wrote on 6 October, 'has been kept in continual alarm for nearly a month, many lives have been sacrificed, trade has suffered enormous losses, every one has been put to great inconvenience, and everything is in much the same state as before the troubles began'. The year 1893 saw widespread rebellions – in Buenos Aires itself, in Santa Fe, in Corrientes, in San Luis, in Tucumán province just down the line from Salta; even, on a modest scale, in Salta itself, where the National Guard had to be mobilized in September. At the end of the month, the railway line at Tucumán was blow up to prevent a rebel advance. A few days later, the British press was reporting that much of the north of the country was in revolt against the fumbling president Sáenz Peña. After this, things became quieter, but still far from stable. In March 1894 the police in Salta had not been paid for four months; in June, the local government appeared to be insolvent, and all the schools had to be closed.

*

Jabez loved the surroundings of Salta. He was overwhelmed by the sunsets. On a walk in June 1894 he saw what he thought was the loveliest sunset of his life:

> A large white cloud hung above the setting sun, which tinged the lower fringe of the cloud with all the colours of the rainbow. After the sun had set, the hue of the cloud changed to a deep lemon or sulphur colour, and then came an afterglow of deep magenta, spreading across the heavens between the cloud and the horizon formed by the mountain tops. The afterglows are very beautiful, differing from anything I had ever seen before. The light is so intense, so clear, so cold, so solemn, sometimes red, sometimes yellow, sometimes a pale clear white, just like an intense electric light.

The mosquitoes troubled him, the fleas even more, and the dogs – every household had them, often dozens, it seemed – never stopped barking. There were also many snakes, and tigers, according to Jabez, sometimes roamed through the woods. But that was a small price to pay for the bliss of the Argentine climate: even in winter the water had never been cold enough to prevent him from open-air bathing.

He liked the egalitarian spirit of Salta. 'This country', he noted in June 1894, after reading effusive obituaries of a great local figure whose relatives were still 'engaged in trade', 'is in this respect truly, and I think delightfully, democratic. Worth and birth, not calling, are the recognized passports into society here. Some very rich people are quite outsiders and some very poor people are welcomed among the best families. The draper and the grocer have just as much consideration as the lawyer and the doctor.'

He was greatly taken, too, with the women, who, he noted, heavily outnumbered the men. 'Courting as we see it in England is quite unknown. Men seldom walk out with their wives and never with their sweethearts. Indeed, the philandering of our lanes and fields is never seen here.' That was clearly not from any lack of temptation: 'The women here have lovely black hair and beautiful white teeth. They seem proud of the former, which they generally plait in two long strings which hang down the back, often to below the waist. But, notwithstanding good hair and teeth, they age much more rapidly than Europeans. They develop early; often marry at fifteen, and are quite mature at eighteen.' He particularly liked the way they dressed in 'brightly coloured shawls and skirts and felt billycock hats . . . as you see them on horseback they really present a very striking picture – all the more striking and picturesque because their dress, with all its brightness, is useful and practical, and not merely fantastic, as is often the case with the garb of the peasantry in out-of-the-way parts of Europe'.

And yet there was so much amiss with the way the country conducted itself. The trouble began at the top. Argentina was overrun by officials and lawyers, and nearly every lawyer was a politician in search of some legal or political post. Yet no one, at national or local level, seemed to stay in a job for long. 'Ardently as office is sought after, it is soon found, as things are now, that it is not worth the having, and the resignations of Ministers, judges, and other functionaries are of almost daily occurrence...During the nineteen months that I have lived in Salta there have been no less than four chiefs of police and three governors of the prison, besides any number of resignations, degradations, and promotions in the lower ranks of the service.'

Sometimes it seemed to Jabez that the solutions were simple. 'Half a dozen years of really purely economical administration, half a dozen years of steady cultivation of individual and local public spirit, and the restriction of the Government to its proper and legitimate functions, would, with the general spread of education and the beautiful climate and fertile soil, transform the Argentine Republic into one of the richest and happiest countries in the world.' At other times he feared the problems were close to endemic. 'The better classes', he wrote, 'are generally very courteous, abstemious, peaceable and lazy, fond of display, and eager to spend every farthing they may get. They go to bed early, get up early too, but have a good long siesta in the middle of the day. I should say they spend about half their time in bed or lying down. No account seems to be taken of time. If you ask any one to do anything for you, he is almost sure to say "Mañana", which means, tomorrow; but the plague is that tomorrow never comes. Indeed, "Mañana" seems to mean "Some other time", "in the sweet by-and-by", rather than "Tomorrow".'

Among the peons, at the bottom of the social pile, there was, he feared, much drunkenness and laziness; also appalling dirtiness and improvidence. But he did not expect the poor to lead better lives until they were treated better. 'I don't think the peons are well treated, or, perhaps, I should say well managed. It is difficult to distinguish the system which prevails here from a species of domestic slavery. They are practically heathens, and I wonder that crime is not more frequent among them. Drink and idleness are their only enjoyment.' Through the Argentine midwinter, he noted, the poor peons lived almost entirely outside their huts, which were mere hovels. 'There is hardly any protection against the cold. You see the poor people crouching round a fire of wood behind any kind of shelter. The children are almost naked, but they seem happy and fat. The women look careworn and much older than they are. Most of them smoke. In fact the cigarette is nearly universal here.'

It was also troubling to a good Gladstonian Liberal – and especially, perhaps, to the son of a woman whose writings had influenced Samuel Smiles's classic treatise – that the people had so little sense of self-help. They wanted everything done for them and seemed quite unashamed of neglect. 'The great blot on this country is its general untidiness. Everything is allowed to fall out of condition and repair... the mortar falls off the wall, or crumbles into dust, and nothing is done to repair or restore it. Windows are broken and doors are smashed; they remain broken and smashed; dead animals rot by the roadside, and they are allowed to rot and stink till the vultures and dogs have left nothing but the bare skeletons. It is the same with the roads: little or nothing is done to keep them in repair and the very site of some roads is lost in the thick jungle of weeds, thistle and shrubs which has overgrown them.'

'Public spirit, as we understand the term, is quite unknown here,' he recorded. 'The people expect the Government or the Municipality to do everything for them, and never think of doing anything for themselves. It is this condition of things, so different to what we have and are so proud of at home, which makes the financial regeneration and political development of the country so difficult. All over England, even in some of our poorest districts, are buildings or institutions or charities, the offerings of pious and patriotic men, who gave of their substance freely for the common good, and thus has sprung up a strong and healthy public spirit independent and even jealous of Government assistance.' In that sense, this was the core indictment of Salta, perhaps. It wasn't Croydon.

These early days with his lady friend in Salta, first in rented lodgings, then in a house he had found for them, must have been almost idyllic. His day began with open-air bathing. 'It is a large open-air bath about fifteen feet square, fed by a strong stream of water coming direct from the mountains. The water runs along a deep trough and tumbles down eight or ten feet into the bath, thus making a splendid douche. The bath is about three or four feet deep, and the water runs out into another trough, and so on to a mill close by. The bath is free to everyone, and is much used in summer. At present (3 July, in midwinter) I believe I am its sole patron.'

With the time on his hands that he had always previously

lacked, he was reading a lot – Macaulay especially – and learning Spanish. Indeed, he'd begun to work on translations, though he wasn't too happy with the results: 'the style is so very different that anything like a faithful translation which preserves the spirit of the original seems florid, and what Velasquez calls in the preface to his Spanish dictionary "grandiloquous", which I think a very pretty word and worthy of the maker of the dictionary'. The clamour in London for his return, the fate of those he had ruined, were far enough away for him to forget them.

But inevitably his pursuers were going to catch up with him and his mistress. It needed, even so, a strange kind of coincidence to uncover their hideaway. 'Wanted' said a poster,

> Jabez Spencer Balfour, late member of Parliament,
> absconded, charged with fraud as a director of public
> company, and of obtaining money by false pretences,
> sums charged in warrants £20,000. Balfour believed to be
> residing in Buenos Ayres. Age 50, looks 55: broad shoul-
> ders, very corpulent; hair dark, turning grey, parted
> centre, thin top of head; eyebrows dark, nose short; face
> full, complexion florid; straggling beard; dark slight
> whiskers, turning grey; dark, slight moustache; appear-
> ance of having weak legs; usually dressed in dark jacket;
> gentlemanly appearance.

Someone cut out a report and picture from the magazine *Penny Illustrated* and stuck it up on the wall of the British consulate in

Buenos Aires. A man down from Salta came into the office and seeing the picture announced that the wanted man was the image of one who was renting his house in Salta.

The British press was immediately after him. Excited accounts, some of them true, appeared of his life in Salta. The monster – the financial octopus, to adopt the image the *Financial Times* had used immediately after the crash, and which now seemed to be breaking out everywhere – who had ruined the lives of the thrifty poor was living in exile, newspapers alleged, 'a life of sultanic luxury...' That was invention: his circumstances were modest. The Freeman sisters had been able to bring him some money collected by well-wishers, and in any case, one could live quite cheaply in Salta. The great champion of temperance, it was further alleged, was negotiating to buy a brewery from a German called Otto Klix, and this, they went on to suggest, was only the start of Jabez's plans to build up a commercial empire in Salta. This politically persecuted English gentleman was apparently about to make Salta prosperous. 'There is no chance of Jabez being given up to England,' the *Buenos Aires Herald* declared. 'He has made the Saltenos believe that he will be a mine of wealth for them. England, if she is really anxious to get possession of Balfour, should offer Salta a loan.'

Local belief in his entrepreneurial benevolence gave Jabez a double appeal. One aspect of it was political, in that he stood for Salta's defiance both of the interfering centralist government in Buenos Aires and of proud, overweening imperialist England; another aspect was economic, in that he would bring employment and reviving resources to a town in danger of going bust. So popular had Jabez become, it was reported, that a new word had entered the language: Balfouristas, supporters of Balfour. His portrait was even featured in advertisements for a local tailor. Such reports inflamed opinion in England. Vituperative newspaper comment was matched by angry condemnation in Parliament. Charles Bignell, a music hall entertainer, was delighting audiences with a song about Balfour: 'a perfect roar of approving applause', one London paper reported, 'greets the lines "We'll find him board and lodging and we'll end up all his cares / He'll get his bloo-oomin' hair cut when he comes from Buenos Aires".'

By August 1893, eight months after Jabez's disappearance from London, some of his victims were threatening independent action. Four of them, the *Pall Mall Gazette* reported, were planning to capture Jabez and take him to a country where an extradition treaty existed. Some £6,000 had already been raised for this enterprise, mostly by a 'leading sportsman' who had promised to furnish a steam yacht. The abductors were well educated and none was aged more than forty. 'If their appearance and their determination – as expressed in the most forcible language – go for anything,' the paper enthused, 'Balfour is as good as once more among us, and with an excellent chance of spending a little time under the same roof as his whilom companions, Messrs Hobbs and Wright.'

The adventure described by the *Pall Mall Gazette* might have sounded bizarre, but what was even more remarkable was that it echoed a stratagem outlined by the poor frustrated minister in Buenos Aires, Pakenham, in a memorandum to Lord Rosebery two months before. 'Another mode of proceeding might be thought of, viz, [Balfour's] sudden arrest by the provincial police, unknown to the national authorities, and shipment on board a British gun-boat at La Plata, consigned to Her Majesty's minister at Montevideo, who would then take charge and send him home in due course. For this, however, great care must be exercised, in order that he should be found to be really residing or staying beyond the federal boundaries, which extend only a few miles beyond the city; that the provincial police will consent to act in this somewhat summary manner; and lastly, but not least, that the Commander of Her Majesty's gun-boat will consent to receive a passenger suddenly placed on board his vessel – apparently under rather irregular circumstances, for conveyance to Montevideo.'

The arrival of this message caused consternation in London. Harassed and harried though it might be, the Foreign Office was not going to endorse a kidnapping. 'I do not think this plan of summary action would be wise or safe,' one official minuted before sending Pakenham's plan on to the Foreign Office under-secretary Sir Edward Grey. 'The plan requested by Mr Pakenham will not do' was the chilly verdict appended by Sir Thomas Sanderson, the Foreign Office permanent secretary. But Pakenham was right: it would take, in the end, something close to a kidnap to get Jabez back into British hands.

The much maligned Argentine Congress, however, had at last begun to deal with its pile of unratified treaties, and in time extradition arrangements with Britain came to the top.

Pakenham's gloom lifted just before Christmas 1893 as the news came from the Argentine government that the treaty was now complete. Immediately plans were laid to seize the fugitive. Pakenham entrusted this task to Ronald Bridgett, who arrived in Salta early in January to take up his duties as consul, which involved looking after his nation's trade interests and the welfare of its nationals living there. ('Mr Bridgett', the *Star* newspaper in London explained, 'is a tall portly man of 50, more or less, active, energetic and with a bluff hearty manner of speaking. He is the brother of Thomas Edward Bridgett, a well known member of the Redemptorist Order.') He used the pseudonym Benson.

On 11 January 1894 Pakenham gave London the news it was waiting for: the Republic's minister for foreign affairs, Dr Costa, had promised that the order for Balfour's arrest would be issued that evening. The Home Office could hardly contain its excitement. 'Has the fugitive been found? Has the warrant been executed?' home secretary Asquith wanted to know on the 12th. 'Please send reply by telegram.' The president had now signed the order, Pakenham reported on the 14th, but it had not yet been put into force, and he added a gloomy postscript: 'Should we ever succeed in effecting the arrest I fear we shall have great difficulty to contend with in obtaining the ultimate extradition, owing to the peculiar conditions of Argentine legal procedure in such a case.' Even so, there was a note of pure triumph in the message Pakenham sent to the foreign secretary on 21 January: 'I have the honour to report the arrest of Balfour, who is imprisoned in Salta.'

With the Argentine police at his side, Bridgett had stopped his man in the street on the morning of 20 January and arrested him. The official version made it all sound quite peaceful. Balfour, it said, had not offered any resistance. That was not how Jabez saw it. For months afterwards, he would rage at what Bridgett had done, vowing to have the issue raised in the British Parliament. The legitimacy of the consul's arrest was angrily challenged in Salta too, as a violent affront to Argentina's sovereignty.

A Balfourista wrote to the *Buenos Aires Herald* describing events on 20 January in very different terms. That morning, he said, Jabez had walked into the city to enquire for letters at the post office. When not far from home he was set on by a body of men who emptied his pockets of all their contents, and took him to the penitentiary, where he was put in a cell without any explanation of the charges against him. Once Bridgett had seen him, he was put in a room with a man charged with murder. He spent the night on the floor amid dirt and vermin and with no sanitation.

The consul had then gone with two others to Balfour's house where they opened his trunks and drawers, read correspondence between him and his family, and even showed these letters to other Englishmen in the town, who were later heard discussing them. And though a judge promptly issued an order forbidding the removal of Jabez's property, Bridgett took what he wanted to Buenos Aires anyway. He couldn't, however, take Jabez too, as he had planned. A prompt application for habeas corpus put paid to that. There had also been a meeting 'to resolve certain knotty legal points', involving not just the governor of Salta, the federal judge, the attorney-general and the minister of the interior, but 'not impossibly the accused himself'. Pakenham was not without hope that before the expiration of many days Mr Bridgett would be able to lodge his prisoner in one of the capital's jails. 'But', he added wearily, 'it is never safe to reckon beforehand on the result of legal proceedings in South America.'

Early in February 1894 an Argentine journalist who used the pseudonym Fiat Lux was admitted to Balfour's presence. He'd been sent by his paper, *La Nacion*, who had sought to make his task easier by equipping him with an interpreter, an Englishman called Bill Thompson. How his managers came to choose Thompson was never explained, but quite early on their journey up country it dawned on Fiat Lux that the translator might turn out to be more trouble than he was worth. It began with a brawl in a station buffet, which left Fiat Lux with a bill for 19 pesos, for one bottle of whisky, two bottles of Pilsen beer, four broken glasses, three broken plates, two broken dishes and one carafe. At a later stop, Thompson, who had gone to inspect the engine, managed to set his clothes on fire and emerged looking charred and shaken.

Every stop on the line produced some new disturbance. At Tucumán station, Thompson enraged the populace first by representing himself as a Protestant clergyman and then by attempting to dance the hornpipe on the platform. All efforts to simmer him down were in vain. He then launched a verbal assault on a café proprietor who had somehow offended him. 'I knew you when you were shining shoes in the Calle Cangallo in Buenos Aires,' Thompson told him. 'Now you think you're a great man. You're ungrateful. Argentina doesn't need you. If you don't like Argentina, why don't you leave, Mr Bootblack?'

Having reached Salta with the erratic Thompson unsteadily in tow, the reporter's first assignment was to measure local opinion, a task which fortunately precluded any need for inter-preters. He found it overwhelmingly favourable to Jabez. The nation's honour, people kept telling him, demanded that Balfour should not be surrendered. 'I consider Balfour to be a great criminal,' one Salteno told him 'and perhaps I would kill him if they paid me well enough, but this does not mean that, because he is a bad citizen, it will be necessary to hand him over without further ado.' Governor Leguizamón was more reserved. 'For some months,' he said, 'the person whom I knew as Samuel Butler has been living here as an individual without attracting anyone's attention, and I am now assured that he is none other than the famous Jabez Balfour, sought by British justice. He was living in a chalet which you must have seen in the Calle Caseros and many people thought he was simply a swimmer.'

A government minister assured Fiat Lux that the fugitive had a comfortable room in the penitentiary where at his request a Bible and works by Shakespeare, Pope and Thackeray had been sent in to him. It was not until Tuesday, 6 February, that the intrepid reporter came finally face to face with his quarry. It was not an easy occasion. He would have to conduct the interview in his very imperfect English since Bill

Thompson, at this vital moment in the proceedings, had disappeared. Gone riding, it was suggested. And the hero of the Saltenos – who had aged and grown thinner, Fiat Lux reported, and was 'toasted by the sun' – was not a happy man. He was dejected at his imprisonment; dejected at his inability to settle his scores with consul Bridgett; and dejected at the absence, just when he most needed consolation, of his inamorata Miss Freeman. The sisters had returned to England shortly before his arrest and heard the news when their ship stopped at Lisbon.

The session with Fiat Lux was brief. Jabez seemed confident that Argentine public opinion had swung behind him as people had learned of the conduct of consul Bridgett. The same thing, he forecast, would happen in England, where he had many friends. He was, after all, no criminal, merely a man accused of a crime, which was not the same thing. Nor had he fled from England in secret, as his detractors alleged: he had come to Argentina for reasons of health. It seemed to him a fault in the decorum of a sovereign state like Argentina that it should seek to accommodate Britain in the matter of an extradition treaty which did not contain provisions for retrospection. At this point Jabez appeared so moved by his plight that he could not continue. He terminated the interview, suggesting they try again the following day.

Bill Thompson, needless to say, had still not appeared. Still, at their second meeting Jabez seemed brighter. This was more like the politician of Tamworth and Burnley, adept at telling an audience what it wanted to hear. He was planning to stay in

Salta, he said. He was buying Klix's brewery. He had plans to write a book describing the province and its wealth of natural resources. 'In this work,' he intoned, 'I plan to show the convenience of English immigration into this province, which, because of its natural richness, its fertile soil and its climate, is one of the happiest provinces of the Republic of Argentina, a country which I greatly admire...'

And yet his admiration had to be tempered because of the way the Republic failed to stand up for itself in a matter which touched on national and local honour. 'It seems quite abnormal to me for a consul of Her Majesty's Government to be carrying out the role of policeman and abusing it, as if the province of Salta were a British dependency,' Jabez complained. 'His easy conversation, his simple but expressive manner, and the way he tries to convince his listener,' Fiat Lux reported, 'left us convinced that we are dealing with a talented man with great intelligence... Balfour [now] was as serene as if he were addressing Parliament... We are sure Balfour will be able to defend himself brilliantly against the tremendous accusations made by public opinion and the press.'

Next up for interview was a neighbour of Jabez, a man called Eugenio Claverie. Balfour, he said, had been trying to persuade him to set up a tannery business with him. Claverie was much taken with this idea, but his wife was deeply suspicious. And indeed, he had had the occasional qualm himself. A well-known inhabitant of the town had approached him offering 50,000 pesos if he would help the fugitive to escape to Bolivia. He'd refused to enter into any such plan. He could not believe, whatever his wife might think, that the plot was of Balfour's devising. He thought it was a trap to catch Jabez – who in any case, he pointed out, could have skipped over the border whenever he chose, without large consignments of pesos changing hands.

Señora Claverie also testified to Fiat Lux. From early in their acquaintance she had feared that 'Mr Butler' was not what he seemed. 'My duty as a wife', she said, 'was to prevent Claverie from becoming partners with a man in whom I had no trust.'

Next, to the famous brewery. Mr Klix was not present, but helpfully his representative Mr Borthwick ('as we understand it, a member of the distinguished English and Scottish Borthwick family...another member is Sir Algernon Borthwick, proprietor of the *Morning Post*') was – and was eager to castigate Bridgett in robustly Balfourian terms for the 'unrivalled misdemeanour' of Balfour's arrest. And then to Bridgett himself. They met in a bar, and before he recounted their conversation Fiat Lux broke off to explain to his managers why their meeting had been so unexpectedly costly. 'We sincerely regret,' he wrote 'that the cognac which we were served was of such a low quality that we did not consider it worthy of a British consul or a representative of La Nacion...There is no doubt that a bad quality would arouse suspicion in the consul, and it was necessary to find a drink worthy of the British representative. And for this reason, Sir, a refined Pellison Pere y ca Cognac appears on our expenses account.'

And so, superior cognacs in hand, to business. Mr Bridgett was unapologetic about Jabez's arrest. 'I don't care in the slightest,' he said. 'I act on a higher order. I represent the prosecutor, and even if I wished to treat Balfour well, I could not tell him so... My conscience is easy, and as regards the unfair accusations, my capacity as a public officer and private individual places me, thank God, above certain persons guided by the incentives of self-interest. You know my country. Do you think they would let Balfour lie on a bed of roses there? The method of dealing with him there would be quite different. Here, Balfour receives certain considerations which, in my opinion, should not be used with a person detained for such a serious accusation.'

This was part of Bridgett's indictment against the Argentine nation: the criminal fugitive Jabez had been mollycoddled. Fiat Lux was quite undismayed. Mr Bridgett, he concluded, was 'a zealous official and a real gentleman'. A better official, perhaps, than some in the service of Argentine institutions: Mr E. Blanco, Salta's active and intelligent inspector of posts and telegraphs, to whom he had been chatting only a few days before, had fled to Bolivia, taking with him the trifling sum of 10,000 pesos. 'Is Salta,' Fiat Lux asked 'becoming Balfourized?'

'Farewell, beautiful town of Salta,' his account of his journey concludes. 'Farewell to the temporary residence of Balfour! Farewell to the home of beauties among the beautiful daughters of Argentina, until we meet again.' On the way home, his train, like Jabez's up to Salta, was involved in a crash. He blamed both the driver, for speeding, and the management, for incompetence.

*

Jabez must have liked what Fiat Lux wrote, despite the reporter's tribute to Bridgett and his failure to condemn the conditions of his confinement, for he had it translated and circulated back in England. But his mood, now Miss Freeman had returned to London, must have become even blacker when he learned of a declaration by the Argentine attorney-general, Dr Kier, which comprehensively ruled against him. Jabez's alleged offences, Kier said, were of such a character as to justify his return under federal law, even if there were no extradition treaty.

The long-suffering legation could not have hoped for a judgment more comprehensively favourable to Britain's case: a declaration of global imperatives transcending narrower national interests. In earlier epochs, Kier wrote – in the Middle Ages, and even in more modern times – when despotism and irresponsibility shed blood in torrents, without distinguishing between the innocent and the guilty, the right of asylum must have been, and was from the Roman laws, a sacred right. But the right to asylum, which had prevented the certain death of the refugees, could not in normal times, and in these times of progress and humanitarian tendencies of modern law, be permitted to obstruct the just and moralizing action involved in the extradition of criminals.

But rulings were one thing: effective action was quite another. As the Argentine winter set in, Pakenham and his team – now augmented by one of Argentina's most distinguished and most expensive lawyers, Dr Lamarca, and also by Detective Inspector Tunbridge and his sidekick Sergeant

Craggs from Britain – were only too well aware of the long way they had to go before their quarry would be yielded up to them. The law in Argentina moved with majestic slowness: there were men in the penitentiary at Buenos Aires who had been awaiting trial since 1888, including one who had testified to having brought his wife to Argentina from Italy to murder her because he'd been told there was no capital punishment there. The *Buenos Aires Herald* wrote about a man called Ross, who having been kept in jail for two years awaiting trial was acquitted, but was then forgotten about and remained in the penitentiary for two years and four months before being released. In London, *The Times* had printed a long piece from a legal correspondent suggesting that Balfour could not be removed. The sympathetic attitude of the Argentine government had nothing to do with the case: in Argentina, it was lawyers who counted. That the treaty of extradition was not retrospective was a very serious obstacle, despite what others had said. Even the news that Jabez was buying a brewery could be a serious impediment: it might open the way to giving him Argentine citizenship.

A Whitehall note attached to the cutting in the file at the National Archive in Kew describes this piece as 'mischievous' and plaintively notes that it seems an odd proceeding on the part of 'the leading English journal' to prompt a foreign law court to pick holes in an English treaty, and to supply a foreign government with arguments for evading its international obligations.

Disturbingly, Jabez even had imitators. A man called Henry Torre Smallpage left the offices of the Pious Uses Trust in Leeds for a holiday. He did not return. Nor did the £1,800 of the Trust's money, which appeared to be missing too. A woman who wasn't his wife travelled with him. Their first destination was Blackpool, from where they moved on to Liverpool, signing in as Mr and Mrs Learoyd. Police enquiries established that they had then left for Buenos Aires. But the ship they had chosen stopped at Montevideo, and there, detectives were waiting. Smallpage, said the *Yorkshire Post's* account of their apprehension, had succeeded his father as an agent for the Trust and was 'very respected in Leeds'.

In April 1894, fifteen months into Jabez's stay in Argentina, came the unsettling news, transmitted from Salta by Bridgett, that Jabez had been let out of jail. He owed this to the return of Miss Freeman, who had made a poignant appeal for her lover's release from custody, mainly on the grounds of his declining health – he was troubled in particular with rheumatism. Either her winning ways or some of the money brought from London had persuaded the authorities to allow Jabez out, at first just for visits, then later to live with his lady under the roof of their friend Señor Alvarado. As the *Times of Argentina* sardonically commented: Miss Freeman had promised to take great care of him and to exercise her ingenuity to help recoup his lost health in order that he might appear blooming, strong and healthy whenever the course of justice needed his presence. 'The Salta federal judge, who appears to be a kind, tender-hearted chicken, allowing himself to be allured by the prayers of Miss Freeman, consented to her petition.'

The first the British contingent knew of any of this was

when someone spotted Jabez in the streets and told Bridgett. The consul enquired at the courts of justice and was told that such excursions were often permitted, though always under the eyes of a vigilante. Bridgett was not much impressed. In his view, such vigilance declined fairly sharply after the first few days. To make things worse he was further informed that the federal judge, who was due to take the next decision on Jabez's future, was unlikely to produce a ruling for a further two months at least. Back in Buenos Aires, the Argentine foreign minister, pestered by Pakenham, condemned the arrangement as 'most improper', but said he couldn't do much about it. 'The whole bottom of the business', Pakenham grumbled, ' has been the old National-Provincial jealousy, and the extreme timidity of the former as regards the latter. Old Rosas [the deposed president of the Republic who had taken refuge in England] would have had none of these qualms and I only wish that in certain respects he were back here now.'

Through the middle months of the year the balance continued to tilt, sometimes in England's favour, sometimes in Jabez's. In April 1894, three months after his dramatic capture of Jabez, the consul Bridgett admitted he had reached the end of his tether. He was no good as a watchdog, he moaned: in matters affecting Jabez, a sleuth hound was required. He feared that a pending judgment from the Salta public prosecutor, a man called Julio Arias, would go against Britain's interests – not least because Arias's brother was part of Balfour's defence team.

The defence had published a case which mocked Kier's pronouncement in favour of progress and international justice:

even higher intelligences such as Dr Kier's, they taunted, were, like the sun, subject to periods of eclipse. Extradition could be ordered only for the commission of atrocious crimes. But the crimes alleged against Jabez were hardly atrocious – some were not even offences under the Argentine code – and anyway were unproved. No action had been pending against him when he left England. The case against him was political.

The defence team also raised the case of General Rosas, which had left Argentina with a grievance against the British which came all too close to touching on Jabez's case. Rosas had taken refuge in England, and although an assassin and murderer, it was argued, had not been returned. 'England today', added Jabez's lawyers, hauntingly echoing London's own words about Argentina, 'is the refuge of the anarchists of the continent.' But none of this had impressed the Salta prose-cutor Dr Arias. The extradition treaty, he ruled, must be taken to operate retrospectively unless there were specific provisions saying it didn't; and this treaty carried no such provisions.

But that did not mean that Bridgett could now get his hands on Jabez. Jabez's lawyers were taking the case to the supreme court. Meanwhile, the federal judge, whose verdict was also expected, still failed to deliver, because of ill-health. By early July 1894 Inspector Tunbridge's patience was reaching breaking point. Though the federal judge could not delay much longer, he warned London, the supreme court was unlikely to take less than a couple of months to reach its decision. 'In this country, time appears to be of no value whatever to officials who draw fixed salaries, and the rule with them is not to do today what they can put off till tomorrow... The only way to get a matter expedited is to bribe every official from the doorkeeper to the minister [vigorously underlined] with whom you are brought in contact.'

Some Whitehall opinion was affronted by this submission, but the new foreign secretary, the Earl of Kimberley, who had taken over from Rosebery in March 1894 when Rosebery became prime minister, was more understanding. 'I do not think Inspector Tunbridge is to be blamed for stating what is perfectly true as to bribery in a confidential report to the Home Office.'

By this time the fugitive had successfully resisted all attempts to remove him for eighteen months. The political pressure in England continued to mount, fuelled by the wrath of the London newspapers. However, much of what they reported was either contradictory or wrong. Jabez had escaped; he'd been freed by the Argentine courts and would never return; or, the courts having found against him, he'd be back in England at any moment. 'Jabez', the *Star* reported on 9 August, 'has been arrested and is even now on his way back to England by boat. There is no doubt', it was saying, a shade less certainly, just a month later, 'that a day or two will see the notorious Liberator organizer on his way to this country in the charge of Inspector Tunbridge.'

Meanwhile there was the ever-fascinating topic of Jabez's lady friend. A surprise was waiting for Jabez Spencer Balfour, the *Pall Mall Gazette* reported enthusiastically. 'He does not know that his legally wedded partner is now on her way to

Argentina, accompanied by her daughter, two servants and a menagerie of cats, parrots and favourite poodles.' The real surprise, quite apart from the parrots and poodles, would have been Ellen's arrival in Argentina. Her mental condition made such a journey unthinkable. As the *Gazette* was forced to admit next day, Mrs Balfour had no intention of leaving England 'even if it were possible for her to do so'.

The end of the Argentine winter had one therapeutic effect. The federal judge was at last feeling better, and he duly pronounced against Jabez. That left just the supreme court to join the consensus. Jabez's fate, at this moment, lay in the hands of his celebrated advocate Dr Manuel Varela; and this was an occasion Varela was ready to milk for all it was worth. He began with a tribute to the wisdom of the Argentine constitution, to be prized far more, as he portrayed it, than the day-to-day judgements of ephemeral politicians. Jabez Balfour had come to Argentina under the shelter of that constitution. He had known that without a treaty it made no provision for extradition, and that even if a treaty were entered into it could not apply to him, since according to Argentine jurisprudence and precedent, treaties could not be applied to crimes committed before such treaties came into force. Of course, had Britain agreed to reciprocity, then Argentine jurisprudence would have allowed his despatch: but without reciprocity, the law rejected retrospection, a principle the Republic had honoured in dealings with Bolivia, the Oriental Republic, Italy and Brazil.

Let the court, the wily advocate further urged, consider the noble example of England, which in the past had so much honoured its laws that it had refused to return 130 slaves who had murdered the master and captain of a ship on which they were sailing. Even faced with a crime of such enormity, the English adhered to their laws. Or take the case of General Juan Manuel Rosas, required by the Republic to answer for his notorious crimes – 'that Nero of modern times, of inexhaustible ingenuity in inventing means for martyrizing, degrading and humiliating the human race'. The laws of England had not allowed the return of even that sanguinary tyrant – and the English honoured their laws.

'The great lawyer', the *Buenos Aires Herald* enthused, 'fully maintained his reputation for profound erudition and unrivalled skill in finding out the weak points of his opponents' arguments and in citing precedents in support of his own.' He did not, however, convince the court, which at the start of November 1894 rejected his case. International obligations weighed heavily with them. It was the duty, they said, of every civilized nation to endeavour to prevent crimes being committed with impunity by obtaining the return of criminals who had escaped their jurisdiction. 'The crime follows the criminal, wherever he goes.' The contention that the extradition treaty did not allow for retrospective action had, in their view, no force. If the Congress, which as it sealed the treaty would have been well aware of its implications for the treatment of Balfour, had wished to exclude retrospective action, it could have said so specifically.

With any other prisoner that might have been the end of the story. But Jabez was not finished yet. He and his Balfouristas fastened on a provision in Argentine law which forbade any person facing a criminal charge from leaving the country. What could be simpler, then, than to muster a team of supporters willing to bring an endless succession of legal actions against the wanted man, thus detaining him in the country while the cases were tried – in practice, indefinitely?

First in the queue was the brewery king, Otto Klix. In negotiating with him, Balfour had masqueraded as Samuel Butler. This surely amounted to fraud. Behind him was Klix's subordinate Louis Borthwick. He had given up a good living to work for Balfour/Butler, he claimed, only to discover to his chagrin and monetary disadvantage that the man was not what he purported to be. As soon as *Klix v Balfour* was out of the way, the case of *Borthwick v Balfour* would be brought to the courts. Behind Klix and Borthwick in this lengthening queue were reported to be five further claimants, one of them talking of bigamy. These were arrestable offences, and they came within the purview of the criminal judge at Salta, the official most identified at the British legation as determined to obstruct the surrender of Jabez. Sure enough, the criminal judge ordered that Jabez be imprisoned to await this series of trials – some of which, if successful, might lead to sentences of up to six years' imprisonment.

Little attempt was made to pretend these proceedings were other than bogus. Reporters from *La Prensa* noted the cheery demeanour of Jabez and his would-be accuser Borthwick. Why not take these proceedings further, asked the *Buenos Aires Herald* – satirically, as it thought. Balfour could, for instance, murder a vigilante. Three days later it repeated this suggestion in a mildly modified form. 'If some friend of Balfour were to call upon him and submit to have his life threatened by Balfour and be robbed by him, then could Balfour remain a prisoner here and not go to England for a long time, and by repeating this lawbreaking from time to time he might live very comfortably as a perpetual prisoner, which is not half as bad as penal servitude in England.'

The authors of this cheerful fantasy were probably not aware that much the same course of action had already been suggested to Jabez. In his book *My Prison Life* he records how just such an approach was made to him. It was one of many such offers during his time in Argentina, all of them involving the payment of £1,000 to 'a certain notability'. The suggestion this time was this: 'On a certain day a particular soldier, a notorious malefactor, was to be posted on sentry duty. I was to be provided by my adviser with a revolver, with which I was to shoot the unfortunate wretch. I had ample opportunities for doing so. I was to be tried for killing him, and even to be convicted. I should then receive a sentence of six years, the longest term of imprisonment in the code of that particular State, with the result that the British authorities would not be able to obtain possession of my person for that period. I was to remain comfortably in prison until the matter had quietened down in England, when I should be released, and could resume my ordinary life in absolute safety.'

To the patent disappointment of his adviser, Jabez expressed horror at this suggestion. He might have come a long way from the Croydon bench and the West Croydon Congregational Church but by no means as far as that. The official meanwhile had another idea in reserve. 'I will arrange for your prison to be broken into; there shall be a carriage and pair waiting for you at the end of the street; you shall be hurried off in the night to a certain estate in the Grand Chaco, where you can enjoy yourself to your heart's content. There is plenty of sport, a nice library, and absolute seclusion. Meantime, I shall pretend to scour the country after you, and when the clamour for you has subsided a little, you can retire to some neighbouring republic in peace.' Both these plans were, 'no doubt, quite feasible,' Jabez wrote, 'but I need scarcely say that I rejected them, and many others'.

Jabez was now beginning his third year in Argentina. For the British legation, the clamour at home and the indignation against the British authorities for failing to apprehend him were quite bad enough already, even without such melodrama. January 1895 – a whole year after Bridgett's arrest of Jabez and the legation's triumphant messages home to London – was as gloomy a month for Pakenham and his colleagues as any in the whole history of this affair. Inspector Tunbridge was ill – ill enough, London papers reported, to be facing immediate retirement. Sergeant Craggs was ill too and awaiting a passage home. Bridgett had had enough and was anxious to get back to Buenos Aires.

Pakenham's hints to his bosses in London that bribery might be the way to dispose of Borthwick and Klix had been vetoed by higher authority. Yet bribery *was* the only way of disposing of Klix and Borthwick. A file of letters in the National Archive charts their deliberations. Money would have to be offered, but offered in such a way that no one would know that it came from the British. For that reason, discussions would have to be conducted in code. Balfour would be referred to as Mills, Borthwick as Beer, Klix as Watch, and Pakenham, as far as one can decipher the relevant note, appears to have been Regina. As the legation could not act directly, their costly lawyer Dr Lamarca would act as a go-between. Lamarca was eager to be involved. 'There must be something of the "stubborn Briton" in me,' he wrote. 'I do not throw up the sponge easily and will certainly struggle to the last.'

Sums of money, it was agreed – perhaps $5,500 for Klix and $3,000 for Borthwick – should not be directly offered but rather floated before the potential recipients. The tactic appeared to work straight away with Klix. Letters reached London in which Jabez complained that the British authorities were using underhand methods. Klix, he said, had been going round boasting that he had been paid $2,000 (notably less than the sum the legation had first considered) to desist from his legal proceedings. Could not some MP be asked to raise the matter in Parliament? 'It is the first time', Bridgett wrote, 'that I ever heard of a man complaining that a charge of fraud was withdrawn, but then Balfour is one in a hundred.'

Borthwick was more of a problem. He was clearly an unsavoury figure, but discerning what he was up to was more difficult. He and Klix, officials believed, were not motivated purely by friendship for Jabez: they were also out to wring as much money out of the British government as they possibly could. In long conversations with Bridgett, Borthwick was frank about that. His association with Balfour had cost him dearly. He had written to a local newspaper rehearsing his woes and the case he meant to bring against Jabez: how two years before he had been lured by this so-called Butler to accompany him to Salta to buy a brewery; how he'd given up a lucrative job with a US assurance company and moved himself and his family up to Salta, only to learn to his consternation that Butler was really 'Jabez Spencer Balfour of noted celebrity'; and how Balfour's perfidy had thrown him back on his own resources. 'Why should I be the only sufferer in this scandalous affair?'

Since he wasn't likely to get any recompense out of Jabez, he told Bridgett, he'd be open to any offer made to him. It would need to be a generous offer, however, since his lawyer was going to take half of it. With Bridgett, Borthwick spoke with contempt of his former associate. Balfour, he said, was an enigma, incapable of straight dealing. His weaknesses were drink and women. In Borthwick's presence he and Miss Freeman had been reading out press reports of the sufferings of Liberator victims and laughing over them.

Bridgett was largely unimpressed with this catalogue. Was Borthwick really so hostile? His information from other local sources was that Borthwick had procured clothes appropriate to a Bolivian woman and offered them to Jabez to help him escape. But Bridgett seems to have thought that Borthwick was right about Jabez's weakness for women. The fugitive, he wrote to Pakenham, would clearly be happy to stay in custody of some kind in Salta rather than be transferred to Holloway or to Wormwood Scrubs, 'where prisoners are not allowed to associate with the "weaker" or "pleasanter" sex'.

Balfour, Pakenham warned London, could well succeed in this aim in this 'fantastical' country, with the help of the money with which he was being fed from London. They could hardly afford to keep a highly salaried official in Salta to ensure that prison really meant prison this time, rather than the status of honoured guest that Jabez had been accorded before. And as it transpired, even the bribing of Klix had not worked, since the Salta public prosecutor, who took the same view of these British manoeuvres as Jabez, announced he was taking over the prosecution 'in the interests of public morality'.

It might be necessary, too, to make contingency plans in case Jabez tried to get to Bolivia, with which country Britain had no extradition treaty. Perhaps by putting men on the border they could catch him and take him to Chile and ship him out through one of the numerous nitrate ports on the Chilean seaboard, from where he could be taken to Valparaiso, and then, ideally, to Liverpool... All this, Pakenham wrote with a terrible weariness, 'should HMG be indisposed to drop the matter altogether'.

And yet, in this darkest hour, salvation was on its way. Salvation in a sharp suit, with a gallery of eye-catching hats and a reputation for getting his man where others had failed. His name was Inspector Frank Froest.

Jabez's parents, James and Clara Lucas Balfour. An apparently ill-assorted marriage – but it lasted over fifty years, until Clara's death in 1878.

Wellesley House: a home and garden fit for Croydon's coming man.

Croydon's first mayor: J. Spencer Balfour, JP, MP – elected in June 1883, and unanimously invited to serve a second term in November. After his trial, his portrait was removed from the wall of the town hall council chamber.

The Revd Dawson Burns: brother-in-law to Jabez and auditor to the Balfour Group. His name on the letterhead was a powerful magnet for the temperance movement.

Where Jabez's schemes were laid: the headquarters of the Balfour Group, Budge Row, off Cannon Street in the City (now demolished).

Jabez's house in Salta, where, according to newspapers,
he was living 'in sultanic luxury'.

Marketplace in Salta. Half a dozen years of good administration, Jabez believed,
could modernize and transform Argentina. He hoped to be there to see it.

The *Illustrated London News* reports the capture of Jabez (27 January 1894).
The British consul, Ronald Bridgett, acclaimed as a popular hero, was evidently a
deft hand with an oar as well.

Señor Boneo
Secretary of the Salta Police

Capt. Hesketh
of the *Tartar Prince*

Mr. A. Peel
Secretary to the British
Legation, Buenos Ayres

Señor Moreira
Secretary of the Salta
Federal Judge

Señor Bavio
Commissary of the
Salta Police

Mr. W. S. Harriss-Gastrell
British Vice-Consul at
Buenos Ayres

Chief Inspector Froest
of Scotland Yard

On April 3 last the Provincial Authorities of Salta finally allowed Mr. Harriss-Gastrell, the British Vice-Consul at Buenos Ayres, to remove Jabez Balfour to Buenos Ayres, under the escort of the Provincial officials, to be there handed over by the National Authorities to Mr. Pakenham, British Minister Plenipotentiary there, for conveyance to England to answer the various charges against him. The above group was taken on board the *Tartar Prince* on April 6, and consists of the five persons who formed Balfour's escort from Salta to Buenos Ayres, and of Mr. Peel, Secretary to the British Legation in Buenos Ayres, and of Captain Hesketh of the *Tartar Prince*

THE EXTRADITION OF JABEZ BALFOUR: SOME OF HIS GUARDIANS

Buenos Aires: Jabez's captors and custodians pose for a celebratory portrait. Given five years to apprehend the fugitive, Inspector Froest (far right) had bagged him in less than five months.

Jabez aboard the *Tartar Prince*: in all ways but one, he told fellow passengers, this voyage was one of the pleasantest experiences of his life.

The Napoleon of finance.
Elsewhere a charmer, in
the City he could be 'a bully of
the first order'.

Jabez in custody after his
extradition. 'Cool and collected, he
looked in the best of health.'

Regina v J. Spencer Balfour, November 1895. Balfour, hand to chin,
listens as his counsel Long John O'Connor (standing left) makes
his doomed appeal to the jury (background). The judge, Mr Justice Bruce,
is at the top right of the picture.

Free at last – but instantly in the clutches of Northcliffe.
The *Daily Mail* prepares the public for Jabez's prison memoirs in its sister
paper, the *Weekly Dispatch*, April 1906.

10

Passenger to Buenos Aires

Return, O wanderer, return

William Bengo Collyer (1782–1854)

'The great detective', Jabez Balfour would later reflect, 'was not an unkindly man.' On the contrary, he was famous for the successes he had achieved by engaging his quarries in affable conversation, lulling them into unwary admissions, and then nailing them before they knew what was happening. Frank Castle Froest was a Bristol man, surprisingly short for a policeman (at 5ft 7ins he was scarcely taller than Jabez), but given to a flamboyance that made him seem larger than life. Though his hands looked delicate, they were astonishingly strong: he could tear a pack of cards in half with them.

Some of his exploits were talked about for years afterwards. Once he pursued a forger on to a boat out of Folkestone and, putting one hand on his shoulder, told him he was under arrest. You can't do that, said the forger: we are now in French waters and you don't have an extradition warrant. I don't care, Froest told him, snapping the handcuffs on. 'You are sailing under the English flag and while that floats above I can do my duty.' A violent struggle ensued, during which Froest called for the captain and asked him to form a court from his crew. The forger, whose name was Cooper, was dragged before it, and subjected to a search that revealed a roll of stolen banknotes and a bag of gold.

Froest had joined the police as a constable in his early twenties and found his way at thirty into the CID. He is said to have achieved the unusual distinction of being reprimanded for an excess of zeal in pursuit of Jack the Ripper. Later he was heavily involved in the case of Adolf Beck, victim of a classic case of mistaken identity, and in the arrest of Crippen, where as head of the CID he directed police operations from Scotland Yard.

Froest was thirty-eight in the year he went after Jabez, and the acknowledged specialist in the recapturing of absconders. Recently he had recently been on secondment to work on what were known as next-of-kin frauds in the United States. Early in 1895 he was summoned to the office of the Metropolitan Police Commissioner, Sir Robert Anderson, and told to pack his bags for Argentina. The Commissioner told him not to come back without Balfour, adding that he would not expect to see him back at Scotland Yard within five years.

In the event it took Froest less than five months – though the credit must be shared with a skilled conspirator, the British vice-consul at Buenos Aires, William Gastrell. The situation that faced them was simple. Very soon the fugitive would have exhausted every known means of appeal to the Argentine federal authorities. There was also a good chance that the Buenos Aires government would now be prepared to take a tougher line than before. The faltering President Peña had

finally been removed and replaced by a nominee of the osten-
tatiously pro-British Julio Roca, a man whose virtues
Pakenham sometimes extolled.

What they had to do now was to find some way of pre-
empting the resolute refusal of officials in Salta, and
predominantly the criminal judge, to comply with what the
government had decided. The course they chose was not
exactly the outright kidnap that Pakenham had once
concluded was the only hope of success, but it was not far short
of it. Indeed, recalling the events for his family in his retirement, Froest used to say proudly: 'I kidnapped him.'

Froest arrived in Argentina early in March 1895. On the
14th, he and Gastrell made the long journey to Salta and
installed themselves in the Hotel Aquila. Their expectation
was that the Argentine fiscal general would rule against
Balfour, who would then take his case to the supreme court,
which would thwart him by backing his extradition. All that
would then be required would be the consent of the minister
for foreign affairs in Buenos Aires, who was plainly ready to
give it. They would then need to seize Jabez Balfour and put
him on a boat back to England before the Salta authorities
could stage their habitual obstruction.

So Gastrell and Froest arranged for the hire of a train and
had it parked in sidings a couple of miles out of Salta. There
was a risk that the news of what they were doing would come to
the ears of the Salta authorities, but the railways in Argentina
had been built by the British and were still dominated by the
British – the station master at Salta was a Briton called

Pettigrew. They also needed the governor of the province, Delfino Leguizamón, on their side. He had long been marked down by the British as a notable vacillator, but here the change of government in Buenos Aires worked to their advantage. Under the new regime the governor feared for his job. While Pakenham in the capital urged the federal government to lean on Leguizamón, Gastrell in Salta suggested he could impress his new master by helping to deliver a fugitive whom Buenos Aires had become as keen as London to seize.

In the meantime, to avoid alerting the Balfouristas, Gastrell and Froest did their best to look like men with plenty of time on their hands, ostensibly happy to spend days out shooting. The notion that the British authorities were putting little effort into their pursuit was reinforced by the clamour in London, where charges that attempts to recapture Balfour had been pursued in a suspiciously leisurely fashion were reaching a crescendo. Could it be that the Liberal government was scared of the secrets that Jabez might spill if he were brought to trial? Reports from Argentina had said he believed his disclosures would bring Lord Rosebery down. Back-benchers on both sides of the House sought to censure the government. Even the celebrated Radical-turned-Liberal Unionist Joseph Chamberlain joined the attack – though as the hammer of Irish Home Rule, his purpose was mainly to dramatize the tensions between Salta and Buenos Aires. This, he warned, was exactly the kind of thing that would happen under Home Rule if such independence was given to Dublin.

Whatever the distant roars of outrage, Gastrell and Froest

had no option but to wait. But for all their apparently casual demeanour, they were on edge. The prospect that Jabez might try to escape to Bolivia seemed serious enough for Gastrell to have 'trustworthy Englishmen' watching appropriate routes. The Salta criminal judge and prosecutor, Gastrell was warned, both had exceedingly bad reputations and were infamously corrupt, while Balfour's lawyer Torino was regarded even by Salta's lawyers as a bad lot. There was clearly no use playing by the rules. Only a snatch would do.

The supreme court ruled on 23 March, but protocol required that the court's decision should now be reported by the Salta criminal judge to the Salta federal judge, and the criminal judge intended to take his time about it. This was also the moment to drag a decision out of the governor. He came to Gastrell's hotel early on the morning of 3 April to say he was willing to co-operate, on one condition. The previous night the governor had been to Jabez's cell at midnight to warn him of his impending decision to support his removal. In the face of the prisoner's protests, he had agreed that Miss Freeman should be allowed to travel with him on the train back to Buenos Aires.

Gastrell was horrified. He was already fairly certain that attempts would be made to snatch Jabez back during this journey. Having Miss Freeman aboard, eager to collaborate with a rescue party, would imperil the whole operation. Yet if he refused the request, the governor would withdraw his consent and wreck the exercise. Gastrell would have to accede.

The Salta court was due to reopen at noon. Word had been

sent from Buenos Aires denying the right of a provincial court to obstruct what the supreme court had ordered, but the Salta officials did not intend to take any notice of that. No service train to Buenos Aires would be running that day, so they thought they had plenty of time to obtain a ruling holding Jabez in Salta. They were unaware that Froest and Gastrell and several federal officials had been mustered at Salta station since the early hours of the morning to await the arrival of Jabez.

The wait was longer than they expected. Time ticked on, and still their prisoner did not appear. A difficulty had arisen which even Gastrell and Froest had failed to foresee. When Comisario Babio arrived at the head of a police deputation to take Jabez away, the official in charge of the prison refused to release him. You've got to do so, they told him, on the governor's orders. The prison official retorted that Jabez was due in court later that day to answer his case against Borthwick.

The stakes were high on both sides. Bridgett had promised $200 to Babio and $50 to every policeman involved for Jabez's safe delivery. A furious argument ensued, at the end of which they agreed to reconvene at the railway station, where the governor would meet them. There they found the British officials surrounded by a loud disputatious crowd, which had gathered as the news got out that the British were trying to take Jabez away. They did not, however, find the governor. He had prudently left for another engagement.

No further debate was permitted. The man who had once been J. Spencer Balfour, MP, was hustled in handcuffs on to the train, Miss Freeman beside him. Moments later it was steaming steadily southwards on its 800-mile journey by way of Buenos Aires towards the London courtroom which had long awaited him.

The question now was not *whether* a bid would be made by the Salta officials to snatch Jabez back, but when. It was left to Gastrell to guard the prisoner and keep a watchful eye on his mistress in the single coach behind. The pro-secretary of the federal judge, two commissioners of police and two sergeants travelled with them. Frank Froest took his place on the footplate, giving the driver his orders. The train must on no account stop. The line had been cleared. In no circumstance must he even diminish speed until he reached Tucumán, 150 miles to the south.

Back in Salta, the local court was convened and swiftly produced warrants for Balfour's recapture and Froest's arrest. It was now not just Jabez's future that was at stake, but the honour of Salta province. A posse was formed, with Louis Borthwick and his brother at its head. The train was moving, as Froest later boasted, as fast as any train in South America could ever have travelled. The heat was intense. He and the driver were black from head to foot, their clothes scorched and covered in oil.

Forty miles out of Salta, anxiously scanning the scene from the footplate, Froest began to discern the posse out on the horizon. Soon they were starting to close on the racketing train. Then they were drawing level; soon they were riding ahead of it. Froest repeated the driver's orders: whatever happens, you must not stop.

One of the posse wheeled away from the rest and positioned himself on the line, waving the warrant and demanding the train be stopped. The driver, seeing the man on the horse was not going to budge, moved to stop the train, but Froest threw himself across the controls and, using the physical strength for which he was famous, forced the driver away. 'No, you don't,' he cried. 'This is a through train.'

The train went through horse and rider, killing them both. It roared on, its speed undiminished, through Metán and Rosario de la Frontera and finally into Tucumán.

There are differing accounts of what happened next. Gastrell, reporting the day's events to his superiors, said that when they arrived in Tucumán no service train was available to take them to Buenos Aires, so he had to hire a second special to finish the journey. But Froest, giving his account of events to a journalist called Frank Dilnot, with whom he later collaborated in writing detective thrillers, said the rattletrap train which had carried them out of Salta broke down, and he had to send for another one. While this was being made ready, a party of local police arrived with an order, wired down the line from Salta, for the arrest of both Froest and Gastrell on charges of murder. Froest found himself in the midst of a throng of angry officials.

The replacement train was steaming into the station. Continuing to dispute their right to arrest him, he signalled to Gastrell to get Jabez and Miss Freeman aboard. The charge was patently incorrect, Froest told them. When the accident occurred he was facing the driver and so could not see what happened. The charge ought to be manslaughter, not murder. As the debate raged on, he slipped outside, saying he needed the lavatory. Instead, he disappeared behind the broken-down train and clambered aboard the replacement. 'The first intimation my Argentine friends had of my disappearance,' he told Dilnot, 'was when we steamed out.'

Later the British government would receive a claim from a Señor Martinez of Salta for compensation for the death of the sheriff's officer, whose name, it transpired, was Chuchini. The accident, Señor Martinez maintained, had been witnessed by a gang at work on the line, who blamed it on the driver's lack of control. Not so, Pakenham wrote to the foreign secretary, Lord Kimberley. According to Gastrell, who after all had been there, the driver had done everything in his power to avoid the accident by blowing his whistle, 'which however was persistently disregarded by the man, who fell a victim to his own folly and carelessness'. It might, however, he counselled, in the interests of avoiding opprobrium, be appropriate to offer a small sum to the family of the deceased, to which he would be happy to make some contribution himself. This was done, in a letter that stipulated that the payment admitted no responsibility, and the $50 offered was to cover both the man and the horse.

Held overnight in the federal penitentiary at Buenos Aires, Jabez was due to be handed back in the morning to Gastrell and Froest. As at Salta, the arrangement came unstuck. When they went to the penitentiary to look for him, they found he had been taken straight to the boat on which he was scheduled to sail to England, the *Tartar Prince*, where Captain Hesketh refused to sign for him. Only when Froest and Gastrell hurriedly arrived did the captain agree to take him.

With Miss Freeman still in anxious attendance, Jabez was taken to the captain's cabin and told to strip to be searched. He refused – in protest, he said, at the presence in the room of attachés from the embassy 'and other loafers'. Her lover's humiliation left Miss Freeman so distressed that she had to be escorted away in tears. In the event, she left Buenos Aires before he did, taking the *Duca de Galliera* to Genoa, travelling overland to Le Havre, taking the boat to Southampton and making her way home to her mother in Wimbledon. She had to sell her jewellery to pay for the voyage.

For a further four days, the *Tartar Prince* was unable to move, first because of low tides, and then because of the weight of 2,400 sheep also making the journey to Britain. That gave the forces of the Salta criminal judge their chance to make another attempt to recapture Jabez. Two men who said they were lawyers acting on his instructions got aboard the boat, flourishing documents, and demanded that the prisoner be returned to them. Inspector Froest, having organized a detachment of crew and some of the rougher passengers to come to his aid if necessary, examined the documents. Turning them upside down, he presumed they must be in Spanish, a language he could not read.

The boarders left the boat, threatening to come back the following day with reinforcements. When they did, they found the boat had gone. Though still unable to sail, the captain had moved it to another part of the harbour. Finally, on 10 April, the *Tartar Prince* was able to put out to sea.

The news that Jabez was on his way home brought general jubilation in Britain. There were cheers on all sides when it was announced in the Commons. Some of his victims began planning to give him a hostile reception. The Northampton radical Henry Labouchere, whose company Jabez had once so enjoyed along with Bradlaugh's on a railway train, published in his magazine *Truth* a poem to mark the occasion:

Bring him straight, O gallant vessel
    Bring him safely we implore,
With the stormy billows wrestle
    Till thou land'st him on our shore.
Let no chance mishap delay thee,
    No cross currents foul thy track;
Keep 'full steam ahead' we pray thee
    Till thou 'st brought our Jabez back!

Freighted with thy precious cargo,
    Which thou bringest o'er the sea,
May no species of embargo
    Of King Neptune's hinder thee!
May no hurricane assail thee!
    May no fog-fiend thee attack!
May thy bunkers never fail thee
    Till we see our Jabez back!

Blow, ye winds, to help the liner!
　　Blow with gusts extremely strong!
Swiftly to our coasts consign her,
　　Blow the *Tartar Prince* along!
Breakers! Stay your angry bluster;
　　And ye storm clouds grim and black,
Cease ye in the heavens to muster
　　Till we've got our Jabez back!

Skipper! Use thy best endeavour;
　　Spare no effort, we entreat.
Seamen! Strive as you strove never
　　'Record' passages to beat.
Stoke, ye stokers, till the boilers
　　Do – well, anything but crack;
Toil away, ye grimy toilers
　　Till we've got our Jabez back!

Hold him tight, Inspector Froest,
　　On no normal care rely,
See that where he goes thou goest
　　Ever keep on him an eye!
'Tis in thee, perforce, our trust is.
　　Be not, then, remiss or slack
Till into the arms of Justice,
　　Thou hast brought our Jabez back.

11

Here's Jabez

The old security is gone
In which so long we lay

Karl Johann Philipp Spitta 1801–59
(tr. Jane Borthwick 1813–97)

Till we get our Jabez back. At some point in this story the trappings had fallen away and J. Spencer Balfour was simply, once again, Jabez. 'Where's Jabez?' his distraught creditors had shouted when his son or his incoherent underlings were produced at meetings. 'Here's Jabez' the crowds would cry on the quayside at Southampton and at Bow Street as his police conveyance arrived for the trial. Going home on the *Tartar Prince* he was, in an odd way, both: J. Spencer Balfour, MP, as he held court among the passengers, regaling them with his stories, or inviting them into his cabin for games of chess; Jabez as he brooded disconsolately in his cabin on the fate that awaited him. The children on board particularly took to him, the *Graphic* reported: 'hypothetical moral obliquity weighs even less with childhood than personal appearance'.

'He is the nicest gentleman I ever met,' one disembarking passenger told the *Daily News*. Still a gentleman, despite his privations, and there were plenty of those: handcuffed for much of the time throughout the voyage, taking meals on his own – meals which were cooked to a different dispensation from everyone else's, because Inspector Froest lived in constant fear that his prisoner might use a knife or a fork to make an end of himself. Had Miss Freeman not said that Jabez would never be brought home alive? The inspector was taking no chances. He had even had a hole cut in the wall between Jabez's cabin and his own, to keep his prisoner constantly under review. There he could see what the rest of those on board could not: Jabez lolling in his bunk, in pyjamas, 'a picture of slovenly corpulence' (*News of the World*). Then the genial good humour, the unstinting courtesy which had him constantly sending notes of commendation to the captain and crew, could lapse and give way to a natural despondency as he contemplated his coming transition from J. Spencer Balfour, JP, dispensing justice, to Jabez Balfour, having to answer to it. 'He was very affable and cheery', one passenger told a reporter, 'though once he was seen to weep.'

On a fine summer morning in May 1895, one month and one day after leaving Buenos Aires, the *Tartar Prince* sighted Southampton. The town was swarming with pressmen. Some had stayed up all night, while others were roused at 4.30 a.m. to be told that the *Tartar Prince* was now passing Hurst Castle on the Hampshire coast, and the boat they had hired to follow it in would shortly be ready to leave. Jabez was woken at six, and appeared on the deck 'looking a picture of health, happiness and contentment'. In all ways but one, he told fellow passengers, this voyage across calm seas had been one of the pleasantest experiences of his life. (It had not been as calm as he claimed, however: some of the contingent of 2,400 sheep had been lost in a storm off Las Palmas.) He even confessed to having enjoyed the company of his captor: indeed, he said, had Inspector Froest been sent out from London earlier, he would have come back long before now.

It remained to shake hands with the captain and crew, to sink a scotch, and to write yet another letter of commendation. Fond farewells were one of his specialities. A month earlier, he'd despatched one to the people of Argentina. 'Before leaving the Argentine Republic,' he had written grandiloquently to *La Nacion*, the newspaper of Fiat Lux, 'I think it is my duty to thank you and the whole Argentine Press, as well as the Argentine people, for the sympathy and courtesy shown me in this country…I can say for myself and my family, that we have never heard a single offensive word. The best test of the culture and civilization of a nation is its behaviour towards ladies and foreigners; and in this respect a distant province like Salta can undoubtedly compare favourably with the most enlightened countries in Europe. The prosperity and progress of the Republic have my most earnest wishes. I beg my Argentine friends not to forget me, and I start for Europe with the hope of returning to this land and of passing here the last days of my life.' 'I salute the editor,' the message concluded.

In a further despatch, to the *Times of Argentina*, he promised that on returning to Britain he would fully account for all the money missing from his companies. He was certain that, with these losses clearly explained, public opinion would materially change in his favour. Now he told Captain Hesketh: 'I have travelled abroad a great deal, but I have never been on board a more excellent seagoing ship than the *Tartar Prince*.'

The quayside at Southampton was thronged with eager spectators, and the press were determined to intercept him for interviews before he was ushered on to the London train. But the pressmen were outmanoeuvred, as Jabez was loaded on to a fast boat which outpaced the one they had hired. 'I did not meet a single Press man who saw Balfour from beginning to end,' the man from the *Daily News* reported, thus neatly establishing for his editor that none of his rivals had done any better than he had. But he did find an engineer who had seen him: 'He was a fattish gent, with a brown wide-awake hat, and he wore an overcoat. Down in the mouth? Not a bit of it. He seemed jolly enough, master, you bet.'

The fast boat swept Jabez and his entourage down to the far end of the docks, from where he was smuggled aboard the train without anyone – predatory pressman or vengeful creditor – spotting him. The pressmen on the boat, meanwhile, disembarked too late for the 7.45 train on which Jabez was travelling, and had to come up on the next one. He and his two custodians took their seats in a first-class carriage, the blinds of which were drawn, thus precluding a reacquaintance with the sunlit fields of Hampshire and Surrey. Other passengers, hearing that Jabez was on the train, clustered around trying to catch a glimpse of him, as did others on the platform when the train stopped at Micheldever. 'There was no mistaking his short bulky figure,' crowed one, 'and his pale flabby face and his weak, irresponsible legs.'

The train headed for Waterloo, where the station was swarming with policemen and journalists. But the policemen were there as decoys: the train made an unscheduled stop at Vauxhall, where Jabez was successfully downloaded to a reception committee made up of Mr McNaghten, assistant commissioner at Scotland Yard, Mr White, the traffic superintendent of the London and South Western Railway, Mr Hoskisson, superintendent of the railway company's police, and any other officials who had managed to argue their way on to platform 2 at Vauxhall. His reception committee at Waterloo had to be content with his luggage, which mysteriously contained a large number of cases each bearing the number 50.

From Vauxhall, the Great Liberator was driven in a four-wheeler across the river, past Whitehall Court – a painful moment, for Whitehall Court was one of his most cherished creations and contained the home from which he had fled nearly two and a half years before – and on to Bow Street by a devious route designed to avoid assembled protestors. As the carriage reached Bow Street at half-past ten, there rose from the crowd, now augmented by people who had missed him at Waterloo, a cry of 'Here's Jabez'. Though some in the crowd were angry and frustrated, others were simply there for the public show. 'Wot 'as 'e done?' asked a woman within earshot of the *Pall Mall Gazette*'s reporter. 'Wot's 'e done?' a man beside her replied. 'God save the Queen! What 'asn't 'e done? I can't say as I rightly remember all the rights and wrongs about it myself. But I know as 'e was a Dissenter, and I know as 'e ruined many.'

Inspector Froest arrived, 'looking bronzed and in the pink of condition' and wearing 'a swagger suit of grey and a grey felt sombrero which anyone less scrupulously particular about the truth would swear was three feet in diameter from brim to brim.' Some late arriving bystanders thought he was Jabez. When a young woman appeared, a cry went up of 'Miss Freeman!', though it wasn't. Another celebrity recognized by the crowd was H. M. Stanley, accompanied by his fellow explorer Anton Greshoff. Stanley's interest is nowhere explained: it may have been a journalist's curiosity, but it may have been partly political. He had stood as a Liberal Unionist against Jabez's lieutenant Coldwells at Lambeth in the general election of 1892, and been beaten. He would win the seat in the general election which was now just two months away.

At last the court was ready. 'What is your name?' the prisoner was asked. 'Jabez Spencer Balfour,' he replied in what the man from the *Star* called 'a fat voice'. He was represented by an Irish Nationalist MP – one of his closest friends in his days as MP for Burnley – called John O'Connor. Six foot six, garrulous and disorganized, he soon began to get on the wrong side of the court, as he would do in all the subsequent proceedings. The charges were read to the prisoner: fraudulently quitting England and taking with him banknotes worth £400; defrauding the House and Lands Investment Trust, on his own account and in conjunction with the already imprisoned Hobbs and Wright, of sums amounting in all to £20,000; defrauding the

Building Securities Company Limited of £1,500. The hearing lasted only a matter of minutes. Then Jabez was taken down to begin his journey to Holloway.

'Picture my feelings,' he wrote more than a decade later, in *My Prison Life*. 'I had had a day of intense excitement and emotion; the arrival at dawn at Southampton; the detectives in their launch; the escape from the newspaper people; the rapid journey through the green field and landscapes of England, looking then at their best in all the brightness and freshness of early spring [though he could not have seen very much of them since the blinds of the carriage were drawn]; the newspaper placards, with the words, "ARRIVAL OF JABEZ BALFOUR"; the first appearance in the dock; the crowded court, and the absence of any friend save Mr O'Connor; and then the Black Maria!'

That journey to Holloway haunted him for the rest of his life. The vehicle was packed, he says, with 'the refuse of the London police-courts', all well acquainted and on excellent terms with their jailers, and talking the language – the slang, he calls it – of prison life. 'I shall never forget that ride through London. It was the last stage in a long and very distressing journey from the slopes of the Andes to the banks of the Thames. I had been a prisoner in trains in South America; on an ocean steamboat; in another train in England; in a four-wheeled cab, and in a police-court; but the ignominy and humiliation of that ride from Bow Street to Holloway, accompanied by the oaths and obscenities of my fellow-travellers, are stamped indelibly on my brain.'

A sense of suffocation overwhelmed him. People who in his previous existence he would only have encountered pleading before him were now on his level. 'To a man of refinement the sudden association, on terms of equality, for the first time in his life with the noisy and ribald dregs of criminal and outcast London is an experience calculated to beget despair even in the most sanguine mind.'

He seemed brighter when he returned to court on Thursday, 9 May. He bowed and smiled with great affability – one gentleman greeting another – as the magistrate, Sir John Bridge, took his seat. Sir John was courteous but cold. The press was again out in force, with the sketch-artists busy: they included Harry Furniss, who had once drawn for *Punch* a picture of Jabez asleep at the height of a tense debate in the Commons, and even the artist who had provided the picture used in his 'Wanted' notice. The proceedings again were perfunctory, with O'Connor making a doomed appeal for the hearings to be stayed until missing documents arrived from Argentina. Liberator victims were out in force and cheered when this request was refused: Jabez, reporters noted, was visibly flustered by their response.

On that Monday the court was unbearably hot and the magistrate half an hour late. Jabez, as the evidence against him unfolded, was taking copious notes. 'Give him five minutes', wrote the *Star*'s reporter, 'and he could talk Sir John Bridge into believing that the past year had been one of unexampled prosperity with all the companies of the Balfour Group, and that a dividend of 10 per cent might with safety and propriety be declared, after leaving a substantial sum to be added to the reserve account.'

The purpose of these proceedings was to establish a case for Jabez to be sent for trial. That outcome was never in doubt. Much of the hearing had to do with a man called Octavius Greig. At first the investigators who came across Greig presumed him to be an invention, but in time they traced him to the fish farm he ran in Devon. The involvement of Greig, a distant relation of Granville Wright's wife, dated from one of Jabez's pet acquisitions, Whitehall Court. The entrepreneur Jonathan Carr, best remembered today as the creator of the West London garden suburb Bedford Park, had set to work on Whitehall Court but by December 1885 was too deep in debt to complete it. Would Jabez come into the project with him? He wouldn't, but he might take it off his hands. Carr was happy with that, and willing – so Jabez later alleged – to pay him a fat commission. Jabez refused the commission but agreed to the deal. After tortured negotiations the House and Lands Investment Trust bought the property for £57,500. The purchase price entered up in the books, however, was £20,000 more than that. The missing £20,000, the prosecution alleged, had been split between Jabez and Wright. To disguise what they had been up to, they invented a fictitious transaction with Greig.

One day in 1886 Greig was ushered into the City office of his apparently respectable relative and asked to sign his name on a piece of paper. Its contents remained a mystery to him, but Wright told him not to worry, since no risk was attached in signing. So he did; and thought no more about the matter until the Official Receiver's findings brought Inspector Tunbridge to his door. Like so many of Jabez's dodgy transactions, this one would probably never have come to light but for the crash. There was also the matter of properties in Wichita, Kansas. This was a venture in which Jabez had been partnered by a peer called Lord Sudeley – 'a short, commonplace looking man,' a court reporter recorded, 'with grizzled hair and a short clipped beard, who resides at Ham Common'. The secretary of the Building Securities Company, Mr Tarver, first learned of this enterprise when Jabez required him to pay over £10,000 of the company's money to buy shares in the Peel Investment and Improvement Company. Like most of Jabez's minions, Tarver obeyed, but the shares were not produced and it later transpired that Jabez had spent only £7,000 on buying the shares and had kept the rest.

The hearings lasted seven days. Jabez, for most of the time, sat plump and smiling – 'a man perfectly satisfied with himself' as one reporter put it. Long John O'Connor, living up to his reputation for exceptional wordiness as well as for exceptional height, was garrulous and was frequently rebuked by the magistrate. Sir John Bridge was frigidly patient. As detail piled on detail the pressmen grew bored. On 17 May, to the relief of most of those present, the proceedings were over and Jabez was committed for trial at the Central Criminal Court – a destination later changed to the High Court on the grounds that the accused was unlikely to get a fair trial in front of a common jury.

His stay at Holloway was more privileged than what would follow: his own clothes, not prison uniform, and the best food he could buy in. A fellow prisoner, detained for debt, cleaned his room and made his bed for 6d a day. But his gloom that summer of 1895 was deepened by a further calamity in the life of his daughter Clara.

Her first marriage, at nineteen, in April 1887, to Walter Ross Bishop, son of one of Jabez's Croydon business and political associates, twelve years older than she was, had ended in June 1888 with his death, six weeks after the birth of their son. Fourteen months after she had come on her proud father's arm to West Croydon Congregational Church to be married, she returned for her husband's funeral. On the other side of the road from the house where they started their brief married life, there lived a man called Perkins William Perkins Case, a doctor, a Liberal, and an aspiring Croydon councillor, thirteen years older than she was. On 13 May 1891, after almost three years of her widowhood, he and Clara were married. They had a son (named Spencer Balfour Perkins Case) and a daughter. Now, in his cell at Holloway, Jabez learned that Clara had been widowed again. At the end of the first week in June, while Clara was in Devon visiting relatives, Dr Perkins Case developed what he thought was no more than a cold. It turned to pneumonia, and on 12 June, before Clara could get back to Croydon, he died at the age of forty-two. Clara had just passed her twenty-eighth birthday.

Jabez's trial, originally set for June, had by now been deferred until the autumn, prolonging the agony. But on 25 October, the court was at last assembled for the case of *Regina v Balfour and others* – the others being his old associates Brock, Morell

Theobald and Dibley. Mr Justice Bruce, a former Tory MP, who had served in the Commons while Jabez was Liberal member for Burnley, had charge of the proceedings; the Attorney-General led for the prosecution; Mr O'Connor, a junior barrister pitched against the might of the English bar, appeared for Balfour. The great advocate Marshall Hall appeared for Brock and, like John O'Connor, took only a nominal sum for his services. The court was packed in the expectation of what one newspaper promised was destined to be one of Britain's greatest trials. That was a bold claim, however, in the year that Oscar Wilde, having lost his case for libel against the Marquess of Queensberry, was arrested, put on trial for homosexual activity, and sentenced to two years' hard labour, and not, as it would transpire, a reliable one.

12

The Octopus at Bay

Who shall dream of shrinking
By our captain led?

Henry Alford (1810–71)

The outcome of the trial had, in effect, been decided already. One way or another – in the revelations of the Official Receiver about the state of the group's finances, in hearings in civil and criminal courts which had ruthlessly exposed the nature of Jabez's operations, in the public outrage over his flight and the clamour for his return, in the angry cries of his ruined victims, in the breakdowns and the suicides counted among them – Jabez's fate was sealed. Having been tried and convicted at the bar of public opinion several times over, he could only hope that the judgment of the High Court would prove to be rather more merciful than that of most of his fellow countrymen.

The main elements in the framing of the popular indictment were these. The Official Receivers, Stewart and Wheeler, had painstakingly pieced together the true, appalling picture of the state of the Liberator and the Balfour Group's finances. Wheeler made his findings available to the journalist Arthur

Spender of the *Westminster Gazette*, which in November 1893 published a masterly dissection of Balfour's operations, drawing both on investigations of how his devices worked and on the recollections of those who had dealings with them. In his opening, Spender drew on the irresistible image of Balfour as octopus or devil-fish, as described in Victor Hugo's novel, *Toilers of the Sea*.

'The octopus', Spender wrote, 'is not enormous like the whale, nor horned like the rhinoceros; it has no dart like the scorpion, nor jaws like the crocodile. The devil-fish has no menacing cry, no breastplate, no claw, no nails, no prickles, no sword, no poison, no beak. Yet of all creatures he is the most formidably armed. In its softness and craftiness, and above all, in its terrible suckers, is the strength of the octopus.

'The octopus is soft – soft and flabby. Its form when not in action has nothing terrible about it ... You may meet it and not be afraid ... And the octopus is crafty. When its victim is unsuspicious, it opens suddenly and holds him in its grasp, till the life-blood is sucked up. The spectre lies upon you; the tiger can only devour you; the devil-fish sucks your life-blood away. He draws you to him, and into himself; while powerless you feel yourself gradually emptied into the creature's pouch ... ' Such lurid imagery, in words and pictures, was commonplace as Jabez awaited his trial.

The language of legal proceedings was more mundane, but still capable of working up popular hatred of Jabez. Hobbs, the builder, and H. Granville Wright, the solicitor, whose arrests had precipitated his flight, had been put on trial in March 1893, with

George Newman, the group surveyor, later joining them in the dock. The judge was Sir Henry Hawkins. The jury, to the delight of the press, included a man called Henry Irving (the famous actor of the same name had recently staged a special performance before the Queen of the melodrama for which he was famous, *The Bells*). Hawkins, true to his reputation for rigour, required his court to sit on Saturday, which the press resented, as did the jury: Henry Irving, the *Star* reported, looked particularly fierce and mutinous.

Hobbs and Wright were charged with forgery and conspiring to obtain money by false pretences from the Liberator and the LAC, and conspiring with Balfour to obtain money from the H&LIT. Wright and Newman were charged with similar offences against the Liberator and Hobbs & Co., while Newman alone was accused of converting £27,000 which belonged to his company to his own use. The evidence against the three men was overwhelming as their subordinate Kentish, Hobbs's brother-in-law – not an ideal witness, in that he admitted to taking a slice of the proceeds himself, but he was still believed by the jury – described how he had helped Hobbs and Wright to cook the company's books, while Julia Hobbs, wife of a cousin of Hobbs, disclaimed all knowledge of transactions made in her name. It took the jury twenty-five minutes to arrive at verdicts of guilty for Wright and Hobbs, while in the case of Newman it did not even retire. Hawkins compared the three to the scribes and pharisees who made long prayers in the synagogue that they might more easily devour the houses of widows. Hobbs and Wright were jailed for twelve years and

Newman for five. None of this, said the *Star*, the newspaper which Jabez had once attempted to buy, would do anything for Balfour's victims: 'the only satisfaction is that the mask of hypocrisy has been torn from the face of a sanctimonious impostor, and that the world is the better for a time by having at least two rogues fewer to deal with.' 'It requires', said *The Times*, 'a rather a high degree of connoisseurship to distinguish the shades of rascality in this precious trio, but upon the whole the palm for consummate scoundrelism must be awarded to Wright.' But the greatest scoundrel of all had evaded justice.

The view in Croydon afterwards seemed to echo that. Wright, that small, weazened, irascible man who rarely now frequented the borough, had deserved what he got, but Hobbs had been hit too hard. The Liberal paper, the *Advertiser*, would reflect at the end of 1895, when Balfour was sentenced, that the term of imprisonment set for Hobbs was scarcely shorter than that for the master fraudster himself. Hobbs was the working man who earned the money which his colleagues then appropriated, and although he was culpable he was no more so than some who had been given far shorter sentences. What was more, it was clear from Balfour's trial that some of the money Hobbs had been accused of appropriating had in fact been split between Balfour and Wright. Hawkins had woefully exaggerated Hobbs's guilt, and the sentence imposed upon him was shockingly severe.

Hobbs's fate seemed all the more miserable in that his motherless daughter of sixteen, Bertha, who had been plagued by illness through her childhood, had been struck down, a week or two after the police had come to Norbury Hall to arrest him, by what was described as 'a mystery illness' and had died a few days after Christmas. Croydon's complaints did not go unheeded. In 1896, Hobbs's sentence was cut from twelve years to eight, and he did not serve even that, being freed two years later because of ill-health. He still owned Norbury Hall and after his imprisonment lived on there until 1914, when he died at the age of seventy.

A second phase in the unmasking of Jabez was a case of misfeasance brought against a collection of the auditors and directors of the London and General Bank. They included some familiar names in this story, like Brock and Dibley and William Theobald, as well as other old Balfour stalwarts like Samuel Pattison, first chairman of the Liberator, now in his nineties, and poor William Blewitt, now recovered from his attempt to kill himself immediately after the crash. Also arraigned were Theobald's fellow auditor Timms; yet another Croydon municipal government man, Alderman Layton, who had left the group well before the crash because he thought its level of funds was inadequate; and two bit-part players called Walker and Revett. The point of these proceedings was to make them pay for some of the moneys lost under their stewardship, which, in a judgment given just before Christmas 1894, Mr Justice Vaughan Williams duly told them to do.

Mr Registrar Emden, meanwhile, had carried out long and searching inquiries into the failure of the H&LIT. Finally, five of Jabez's closest lieutenants – Brock, Dibley, Coldwells, Morell Theobald and Wright's brother, the major – faced committal proceedings, long delayed in the hope of the skipper's return but finally begun in February 1895 when it seemed there was little hope of getting him back. This, ironically, was the month of Frank Froest's journey to Buenos Aires.

Because of its importance the trial was moved from the Mansion House, where the City court usually sat, to the Guildhall. It opened without George Dibley: too ill to attend, said his doctors, with diabetes. His condition was described as 'degenerative' but some hope was held out that he might attend when the weather was warmer. He arrived on day six, looking weak, and heavily swaddled with a rug wrapped over his knees.

The charges against the defendants varied from case to case but all had to do with false entries in company books and issuing statements designed to mislead investors. A vast and melancholy body of evidence dealt with people and projects already familiar: the extravagant triumph at Brading Harbour, the convenient property valuations of Binfield Bird, the entanglements of the companies, the sales of properties at Romford and Ilford and elsewhere, which seemed to have no purpose except to cheat and mislead.

That Mr Alderman Horatio Davies, presiding, would send the defendants for trial was never in doubt. Indeed, he could not contain his impatience, announcing on day seven that a prima facie case had been made against Brock, Dibley and Theobald, though less so against Coldwells and Major Wright. But you haven't heard all the evidence yet, defending counsel protested. All he was saying, the alderman told them, was that he was 'minded' to send them for trial – but he still had an open mind. Mr Atherley-Jones, a radical MP and son of a Chartist leader, who was representing Morell Theobald, said the alderman's position made further cross-questioning point-less (though being a lawyer, the words he actually used were: 'an act of supererogation') so he wouldn't bother in future. In any case, his client had a most complete answer to all the charges against him (laughter in court). The hearing lasted fourteen days, at the end of which all the defendants were sent for trial, and bailed on terms which some complained were excessive.

Meanwhile, raising the temperature still higher, a non-conformist minister called J. Stockwell Watts, who was acting as secretary of the Liberator Relief Fund, published savage denunciations of Balfour, interspersed with poignant accounts of his victims' sufferings, which newspaper reports augmented. Here, garnered by Watts, was the testimony of one ruined woman, whose fear of the workhouse was a perpetual theme of such letters: 'Every penny of my money was in the Liberator, £1,200. The interest paid my rent and taxes, and with the help of that I was able to get my living in a small private school. I am 55 years of age, and have worked as hard as any woman could since I was 17 ... Unfortunately for me, this trouble, with its sleepless nights of racking anxiety has so crushed me – some days are dragged through in agony – my future is dark enough, I know not in the least what will become of me. I can only sob out in the night (the only time I can allow myself the luxury of crying). Oh God, I have worked so hard, and looked forward to my little home, with my books, so longingly, save me, oh save me from the workhouse.'

A succession of press reports filled out the picture. Emily Ekins, a maiden lady of seventy from Huntingdonshire, was found by a coroner's inquest to have killed herself, her mind having become unhinged by the loss of the greater part of her fortune through the Liberator crash. William Penny, a Peckham bookseller, had killed himself for the same reason. Thomas Henry Pexton of Scarborough, who was thirty-seven, 'took his life', it was reported, 'in a most determined manner'. His wife, worried that he was late for his work in a bank, found the bedroom door locked: when it was forced he was found with his head nearly severed. The couple had four children. Pexton had been depressed in consequence of the death of his mother, who had put her money into the Liberator on his advice. Verdict: death by suicide while temporarily insane.

An interim report from the relief committee a year after the crash examined over 2,000 cases where the sufferings of the victims were assessed as severe. Women, most of them single or widowed, outnumbered men. Nearly half of all victims were over sixty. These were people of limited means but some social aspiration who had entrusted their money to respectable and religious Balfour and his respectable and religious associates in their struggle to keep afloat. 'Single women,' wrote George Robb, in his *White Collar Crime in Modern England*, 'the elderly, clergymen and other genteel, but economically marginal, members of the middle class, were likely to "gamble" with their money in the constant struggle to keep up appearances.' Jabez's claim in *My Prison Life* that 'no one suffered more from the crash than I did' is hard to swallow in the light of stories like these.

Watts had assembled to run the Liberator Relief Fund a committee replete with MPs, City men, and the clergy. Its appeal spoke of 'acute and widespread distress; hundreds of aged invalids; good, honest, thrifty but helpless persons, and numerous widows and orphans . . . suddenly reduced to utter want through no fault of their own'. At least £10,000 was needed immediately to save the worst cases from destitution and fully £100,000 would have to come in to furnish anything like substantial relief. The Queen regretted she could not participate, citing the many such requests always addressed to her, but her son Prince Christian, the one who had turned out for one of Hobbs's cricket matches at Norbury, became its patron.

Not all responses to Watts's increasingly anguished appeals were favourable. 'No,' one writer replied, 'I will not give my hard earnings to perpetuate scoundrelism. If I had been asked to subscribe to the cost of erecting a scaffold on which to hang Balfour, Hobbs and co., and the directors and guinea pigs connected with these scandals, I would gladly have done so.' And a chartered accountant wrote: 'To relieve people from the consequences of their folly is simply to perpetuate folly.'

The calculation of the sums that would be needed to alleviate distress continued to climb and the contributions were never likely to match them. There was competition, too, from other disaster funds – especially that launched after HMS

Victoria came into collision with HMS *Camperdown* during naval exercises and sank with the loss of thirty officers, including an admiral, and 320 men from a crew of 600 in June 1893.

According to Watts – in a challenge soon taken up in the Commons – some in the City were making a tidy profit from exploiting the crash of the Liberator. The liquidator was seeking to maximize returns from some of the group's ambitious projects, such as the Hotel Cecil and Hyde Park Court, whose lavish arrangements had so impressed the *Financial Times*, by raising the money needed to complete them. And who should be in the forefront of those he had turned to for money but the Debenture Corporation, of which Jabez had been a director, and in which his friend and political colleague H. Evans Broad was a powerful influence. For a loan of £900,000, said Watts, this company was taking 6 per cent interest and 10 per cent commission. To Liberator victims, that looked like daylight robbery.

What seems to have driven Watts on, even more than his fury at the evil influences of Mammon, was his fear that the crash of the Liberator – an event which, given the suffering it had inflicted, deserved in some senses, he said, to be regarded as 'the biggest crime of the nineteenth century' – would damage the good name of religion. These were religious people – the Liberator's whole initial approach to the public had been based upon that connection – and here were thousands ruined because they had put their trust in men of religion. 'It has been said,' Watts wrote, 'and not without a little show of truth, that "under the plausible garb of Religion, the worthiest among our working-class communities have been ruthlessly robbed of their thrifty savings", and "the enemies of the cross of Christ" have gleefully pointed at the lamentable fact.' What had happened to them now imperilled faith in Christianity itself. Mr Registrar Emden was also moved to one of the angry outbursts that punctuated his inquiry into the H&LIT failure when told that the directors had at the start of one of their meetings praised God for making them prosperous. 'Shocking – perfectly shocking,' he said.

A particular target here was Dawson Burns, son of the Jabez Burns who had inspired his mother's activities on behalf of religion and temperance, and husband of Jabez's sister Cecil. The resentment directed against him was second only to that inspired by Jabez himself. This was largely because his name, above all the rest, had a special allure for non-conformist Britain, but also because a speech he had once delivered on the duties of auditor had come to be seen as a classic text for the profession. 'What is an auditor?' Burns had asked. 'He ought to be very much like a watchdog; very careful to listen to any suspicious sound; able to bark and perhaps even to bite if it is necessary [laughter]. The peculiarity of his position is this, that whereas the watchdog has to watch those outside, he has to watch those that are inside. He has to take care that those who manage the accounts do their business properly.' These words had been dug out and compared with his account in the courts of his own performance as a Balfour Group auditor. Asked why as Jabez's auditor he had questioned so little, watchdog Burns replied that an honest man did not suspect dishonesty in others without some ground for doing so.

That Burns had left the group as early as 1886 was not enough to exonerate him. The *Pall Mall Gazette* quoted one ruined investor: 'In making our deposits in the Liberator, we knew nothing and thought nothing of Balfour, Wright or Hobbs; but we did know, and have often heard and applauded, the Revd Dr Dawson Burns and his criticisms on the Drink Bill, and it was his name that inspired us with a sense of security, and induced us to invest in a society with which one so acute at figures was concerned.' Burns, said the *Gazette*, must have known that he had been given a place on the board merely because the guarantee of his name might attract the savings of people who lionized and trusted him. His name was a bait to catch dissenters and teetotallers. If Balfour ever stood in the dock, Burns would deserve to stand beside him. In November 1893 reports appeared that the UK Alliance had decided to get rid of Burns at the end of the year. The leadership of the Alliance had asked him to leave two months before, but Burns had refused.

The Alliance, from whose platform Jabez had spoken only a few months before the crash, was one of the beneficiaries of Balfour's largesse which responded to Watts' appeal by returning what it had now come to regard as an ill-gotten gain: the donations it had gladly taken from him over the years. The Congregational Church at West Croydon, to which he had given £1,000 and a set of bells, sent an equivalent sum to the relief fund. The worshippers at Hollingreave Congregational Church, Burnley, sent a cheque for £25, matching what Jabez had given them. The army volunteers at Doncaster, scene of one of his parliamentary candidacies, returned the silver challenge cup with which he had presented them. The East Lancashire volunteers, based in Burnley, had a similar cup and that came back too. The Croydon Board of Guardians debated the removal of Jabez's name from the memorial stone of the infirmary in Mayday Road. The Vicar of Wallington was opposed to this move. Jabez, he said, whatever his faults, had served Croydon well, and in any case, if you started removing from such memorials the names of all who were not virgin white, how many would you have left? Even so, the motion was passed by ten votes to six.

The cruellest insult of all, though, was inflicted by Croydon council, which removed the life-size portraits of Balfour and Hobbs – the only men to have twice been mayor of the town – from the council chamber of the new town hall whose opening Jabez had graced nine months earlier. The picture of Hobbs was replaced by a plan of some cottages. That of J. Spencer Balfour, JP, MP, was replaced by plans for a sewage works.

From this mass of testimony there emerges a kind of composite portrait of Jabez at work, fleshing out the mechanics of how the frauds worked – the fictitious transactions, the ludicrous valuations, and the rest of the repertoire of doubtful devices already reviewed in this book – and making it clear how for so many years he had got away with it. Here is Jabez, dominating every phase of the companies' work, even when, as in the case of the Liberator, he is no longer officially a director; Jabez engineering a change in the rules to allow him to sanction any transaction he pleases.

'Do you agree,' the prosecution asked Wheeler, who as liquidator knew as much about life in the Balfour Group as anyone, 'that Mr Balfour may be described as the life and soul of the party?' 'Yes,' said Wheeler, 'I think that describes the position.'

'Were you part of an inner ring?' Dibley was asked. The only inner ring, he replied, was Jabez. Who sanctioned this transaction? the court demanded of the woebegone Mr Tarver, secretary of the Building Securities Company. Generally, he replied, Jabez arranged everything. 'Everywhere', wrote Spender in his *Westminster Gazette* deconstruction of the Balfour Group, 'we find that tremendous personality dominating and hypnotizing his colleagues, as well as secretaries, auditors and solicitors. He it was apparently who convinced them that all would come right if they only went on boldly.'

The evidence here, unlike that in the courtroom, was not given on oath, but it seems completely consistent with what the courtrooms were told. 'I got to know him first', one of his underlings told the *Westminster Gazette*, 'in his capacity of the "man of business turned squire"; when he kept open house, entertained great and small, and generally did his best to play the role of English country gentleman. There was an air of genial ruffianism about him which was very taking, and an open joviality – somewhat subdued in serious company – which seemed to give the lie to any suspicion of mean or disreputable conduct, and deceived men of more experience than I, but a very short experience of "the skipper" in the City altered that.'

For Jabez in the City, this deponent had discovered, was a

bully of the first order: 'In the City, the geniality vanished and the ruffianism increased.' Here was the side of Jabez, mostly concealed, that emerged in his feud with his brother at Tamworth. In board meetings everything had to be done at breakneck speed, and Jabez ('noisy as ever', his mother had said of him, 'he talks a great deal') seemed to talk all the time. When some director dared to challenge the figures placed before him, asking if they were truly all right, Jabez snapped at him: 'Of course they are! Do you think I would put them before you if they weren't?' He liked to keep people waiting. As they sat outside his office they would hear him, through the door, dictating a letter; then, when he felt he'd delayed them enough, he liked to appear in the doorway, 'like the sun breaking through the clouds, with both hands stretched out, all apologies and welcome'. For those who had dealings with a great twentieth-century rogue, there are inescapable echoes here of the late Robert Maxwell.

And here before these various courts was the pathetic parade of those who knew something was badly wrong but, for the most part, did nothing about it. Here was Morell Theobald, director and auditor, who did get out, but too late, complaining that he fell among scoundrels who failed to reveal they were scoundrels. Mr Theobald, said his counsel in the vain hope that his client might not be sent for trial, was unfortunate enough to become associated with men like H. Granville Wright, Newman and Kentish. Some of these men were now in prison and some others had been proved to be scoundrels. Mr Theobald had believed they were honourable persons, and continued to do so until the subsequent investigations took place. Wright and Pattison, for example, were members of eminent firms of solicitors! Balfour was respected by all who knew him, apparently (laughter), and a member of the House of Commons! Also, his lawyer explained, Mr Theobald was not a well man.

Here was poor Dibley, auditor and director, with his scarves and his rug and his diabetes. He had absolute confidence and faith in the honesty and ability of his fellow directors, he told the Guildhall hearings, but especially in Mr Balfour. Mr Balfour always assured board meetings at which he presided that he'd personally checked all the accounts and nothing was wrong with them. Mr Balfour, Dibley explained to a meeting of creditors of the London and General Bank, held various offices with leading public companies. Moreover he was spoken of as a future Cabinet minister (loud laughter). Dibley himself had known Mr Balfour when he was but a boy, he assured the H&LIT inquiry, and had also known his mother – 'a most delightful woman'. His confidence in the Liberator's operations, he explained, was due to the fact that the son of the wonderful mother had told him all was going swimmingly. He believed that everything was being done correctly and the society was in a good position. At which point a cry of 'What a lie!' echoed around the courtroom and a Mr George Webb, one of many victims attending the hearing, was called up by the registrar and thrown out.

And here was faithful old George Brock of Croydon, at the heart of most of Jabez's operations. His counsel – Sir Edward

Marshall Hall, no less – said, very fairly, that Brock was 'one of a number of poor unfortunate fools who believed all that Balfour told them'. Yes, he had had his doubts about transactions involving Hobbs, he told the H&LIT inquiry, but he did not like to ask awkward questions. 'You shut your eyes to such things?' he was asked. 'I think I was . . . er . . . careless.' Had the auditors, the Theobald brothers and Miall, not warned him at one point that he ran a risk by agreeing to dubious balance sheets? He was sorry, he could not remember. Had he not, a shareholder asked, had qualms when Jabez appointed a clergyman and his tailor as auditors? He saw no reason to question their suitability at that time. 'Mr Brock', wrote the man from the *Star*, 'was a man of large beliefs. He has lost some of them since, and looks quite disillusioned, as he stands in the witness box, swaying himself gently backwards and forwards, and sorrowfully contemplating the paper laid before him over the top of his steel-rimmed eye glasses. "I am not aware of that" he kept saying. "You don't seem to be aware of anything done while you were a director," Mr Registrar Emden broke in. "You give the same answer to everything".'

Old Mr Pattison, the chairman of the Liberator, with his silver tongue and his hazy command of the figures, took the stand, too, assuring the H&LIT inquiry that he didn't take the decisions: he left that to Balfour and Brock and Dibley and H. Granville Wright.

> The registrar: 'Do you mean that in these gigantic transactions you relied on the statements of others?'

> Witness: 'It was impossible to go into so much detail as in smaller matters.'
> The Registrar: 'Do you think that you ought to have continued as a figurehead for the company, the share-holders and depositors imagining that you were carrying out the necessary duties of your position when you were not doing so?'

The court stirred. Mr Pattison thought that unfair. Why, he several times offered to resign his appointment; but Jabez had told him not to.

At which point Mr Need, a depositor, had a question to ask. How much was Mr Pattison paid to be chairman?

> Mr Pattison: 'I think it was £250 a year.'
> Mr Need: 'Did you think you earned that from us working men?'
> Mr Pattison: 'I think so, sir' (laughter).
> Mr Need: 'Well, I don't. I am, a man living on 30 shillings a week all my lifetime, and ruined over it is what I am.'

Major Wright, that upstanding military man, was asked about the society's prospectus. He had never read it, he said.

> The Registrar: 'It is a most extraordinary fact that each director, up to the present, comes here and says that he never took the trouble to see the statements upon which they were getting these immense sums of money.'

The Official Receiver: 'I may take it that you concurred in the issue of a balance sheet about which you knew practically nothing?'

Major Wright: 'You may.'

Among the lesser fry was Frederick Rocke of the House and Lands Investment Trust. 'You thought,' the registrar asked him, 'that if you let a few flats well and saw that the clerks did not play cards, you had performed all the duties of a director?' 'Yes, so far as the House and Lands was concerned.'

Asked how the board had come to agree to the accounts placed before them, Mr Rocke said that Mr Balfour explained them to the directors and his explanations were usually so full that no further discussion was needed (laughter). Wasn't he worried that the Trust was borrowing at such high interest rates? Yes, he was. Did he say so? No. Why not? Because he was much too heavily under the influence of Mr Balfour and believed that what was done by him was for the best. Did he never consider the interests of the shareholders and depositors? 'I cannot say that the matter came to my mind in a concrete form' (laughter).

And then there was Captain Revett, a former seafaring man, director of the London and General Bank. He attended as many board meetings as he could manage, but was terribly troubled by rheumatism. But even when he attended he thought it best not to interfere, as the other directors knew more than he did.

The registrar: 'What was your object in joining the
board?'
Witness: '£200 a year. I had been at sea a good many
years and I wanted something to do. I spoke to Mr
Blewitt and he said there would be nothing to do and
£200 a year to receive.'

Abject. But are they any more abject than the group which
surrounded Robert Maxwell, some later promoted to places of
high authority; people far better educated than Balfour's
associates, more skilled in the ways of the world, yet ready to
swallow his lies and to keep their mouths shut for fear of breaking the pledges to secrecy which they had signed as they took
their fat contracts?

Two other groups in the Balfour brigade were given special attention. One was the guinea pig class: the MPs and lords whose
names looked good on the letterhead. Henry Broadhurst, for
one: a much respected Lib Lab MP, who left school at twelve,
worked as a stonemason, became secretary of the Trades Union
congress and served as a Home Office minister. For all his fine
qualities, Broadhurst had a Revett-like approach to his duties.
He was promised that his appointment, which was 'honorary',
did not involve any work. He had taken it on the specific assurance that he would not have to worry his head with the books or
watch the accounts.

The Liberal peer Lord Oxenbridge, who carried the privileged title of president of the Liberator, appeared to have

forgotten the fact before being rudely reminded of it when the society crashed. *The Times* brusquely upbraided him, though it made the mistake of calling him chairman rather than president. He had failed to utter a word of apology for the catastrophe, the newspaper complained. Indeed, he and his political friends had judged it right at this moment to have his portrait presented to him, 'with all the banqueting and fulsome speechmaking that belongs to such a function'. Oxenbridge wrote back the same day complaining. He had acceded to the request to take up his position because he believed the building society was likely to be advantageous to the working classes. He had never had any reason to doubt the honour and competence of those who managed it. Of course he regretted that now. No one could lament more than he did the suffering that had overtaken so many, but he could not see that he was in any way responsible.

On the contrary, *The Times* replied: he was guilty of 'astonishing laxity'. Thousands of poor people, now facing ruin, had been deluded by his assumption of duties which he had never had the smallest intention of carrying out. Oxenbridge was a typical late nineteenth-century Lord on the Board, a species still much in evidence at the start of the twenty-first century: a survey by Labour Research in 2001 found 217 peers sharing 618 directorships, and 80 peers sharing 135 consultancies – some with business portfolios of Jabezian proportions.

But those who were most vigorously blamed, and deservedly so, were the auditors and accountants. The unqualified nonconformist minister, Teesdale Davies, had his nose rubbed in his inadequacy. He knew nothing about accounts, he confessed, or about surveys or valuations.

> The registrar: 'Do you suggest that you had no responsi-
> bility for drawing up the balance sheets?'
> Davies: 'Only concurring in them' (laughter).
> The registrar: 'Do you think you know what a reserve
> fund is?'
> Davies: 'I think I do'(laughter).

The professionals were dealt with more savagely. The eminent auditor Miall, partner of the Theobald brothers, was asked if he had ever had worries about the inordinate spending of Hobbs. Not really, he said; not after my partner Morell Theobald told me that Hobbs was a progressive builder. He had thought that Hobbs was fully secured though he had not bothered to check. Why, when he and Theobald resigned as auditors of the H&LIT, had they nevertheless signed the balance sheets? To do otherwise, he replied, would only have ruined the company.

A further auditor, Mr Feast, said he did not check the company's deeds as he did not have time. Asked why he had failed to warn the directors about their failure to keep a proper register of securities, he replied: 'I don't know why I didn't, but I didn't.' Thomas Davies, chartered accountant, Liberator director and auditor, said he had signed the 1891 accounts without going through them because he had influenza. He had never read the statement of auditors' duties in the Building

Societies Act, but had only looked to the rules of the Society. That, said the registrar, was the most extraordinary statement he had heard in these whole proceedings.

The directors were bad enough – mere tools in the hands of Balfour, *The Economist* reflected after Hobbs, Wright and Newman had gone to prison. But even more extraordinary, it said, was the conduct of the chartered accountants who had recognized the dangerous courses into which the companies were drifting, but contented themselves with writing protests to the directors, and allowing these protests to be withheld from the shareholders. Mr Registrar Emden in the H&LIT hearings put the same point to the auditor William Theobald. If you'd acted more openly to warn the shareholders of what might be about to happen, you might have averted disaster, he said. Theobald disagreed. Mr Balfour, he said, had such influence over shareholders' meetings that he could carry anything that he chose.

The Economist thought this contemptible, especially in view of the fact that because of their reticence the crash had been so much greater and more widespread than it would have been had they spoken out at the time. It returned several times to this theme thereafter, making the case for reform. The auditors had colluded in hoodwinking shareholders: would the Institute of Chartered Accountants now act? The ICA wrote back to say that these matters were plainly *sub judice*. It did, however, agree that an auditor would have failed in his duty if he had not satisfied himself as to the propriety of the figures a company placed before him; by adding his certificate to the balance sheet, he effectively commended it to shareholders as a true view of the company's standing. Good, said *The Economist* drily. We seem to be making progress.

Again, they were here at one with the excellent registrar of the H&LIT inquiry, Alfred Emden. 'I only hope', he observed as Thomas Davies stepped down, 'that after the extraordinary evidence that has been given in the course of this inquiry it will have the effect of calling the attention of the legislature to the absolute want of protection which shareholders in building societies labour under, in the matter of the management and audit of the accounts.' Advice which was duly taken when Parliament passed the Building Societies Act 1894 – as much a monument to the career of J. Spencer Balfour as the Hotel Cecil or Whitehall Court.

13

The Liberator in Chains

Humbled for a season

Caroline Maria Noel (1817–77)

The court that heard the case of *Regina v Balfour* and others assembled on 25 October 1895, just over three years since apprehensive creditors had found the doors of Jabez's bank locked against them. Mr Justice Bruce was on the bench, with a jury of good commercial men who would, with luck, understand the evidence. The little courtroom to which the trial had been transferred from the Old Bailey was packed. Three-quarters of those who tried to get in were unable to find a place. Nearly fifty pressmen were present, many of whom had to stand; also a cluster of lawyers and Members of Parliament who had been in the House with the prisoner. The other defendants, having been out on bail, arrived first. Then a flurry at the door announced the arrival of Jabez, accompanied by the governor of Holloway and flanked by a warder who confided to reporters that 'him and me are the best of friends'. This was his first reunion with his old friends and collaborators. 'He greeted them with many smiles.' But he did not receive in return: the special correspondent of that old admirer of Jabez, the *Croydon Advertiser*, noted how cold Brock and the rest were towards him.

Balfour, said this reporter, was otherwise cool and collected and looked in the best of health. He wore the same dark, tightly buttoned frockcoat in which he had appeared at Bow Street. He had evidently paid much attention to his toilette. His low collar was scrupulously white, his dark tie arranged in faultless order. He gazed around the court, nodded and smiled at acquaintances, bowed to the judge, who did not respond, and 'generally conducted himself more like a person who occupied the position of a prosecutor than a prisoner'. Brock, the correspondent added, was a tall man with iron grey whiskers, who wore a fashionable plum coloured overcoat, while Morell Theobald, the accountant, bore a striking resemblance to a famous novelist of bygone days (although sadly, he did not reveal which one). Dibley, the henchman of Dawson Burns who had stayed with Jabez after Burns broke his links with him, was a fine-looking man, he said, though of commonplace appearance.

Two others who should have been there were missing. Major Wright, the old Royal Engineer, whose solicitor brother was already serving his sentence, was unwell. There were hopes that he would attend later. The absence of Coldwells, the loyal supporting act on so many of Jabez's political platforms, was more permanent. On 29 July, less than a month after he had finished his term as MP for Lambeth, his wife went into the garden of their summer home in Bournemouth and found him dead on the ground. Two years before, the subsequent inquest was told, he had come through an illness that the doctors thought he might not survive. The strain of the coming trial and the worry of what a civil action against him would cost had been too much to bear. 'I am daily being killed by worry,' he had confided to his son.

A juryman asked an obvious question. Was there any evidence that Coldwells had taken poison? None, said his doctor. The coroner had some sympathy with the questioner. There were infallible tests for detecting the presence of poison, he said, which had not been carried out. He could not feel certain that the jury would wish to accept the doctor's evidence. But it did.

It is an indication of the reach of Balfour's empire and the numbers hit by the crash that the court had trouble recruiting a jury. The first potential juryman claimed to have had extensive business transactions with Balfour. A second said he could not conscientiously serve because he was biased. A third was a depositor in the Liberator. A fourth said his wife had an interest in the companies. A fifth had a brother who had served on the board of the Liberator. All were dismissed, along with a sixth who, for reasons not blamed on Balfour, was deaf in one ear. It seemed for a moment as if no reserves were available, but court officials assured the judge they were there: they could simply not find a way through the crush of people trying to get into the courtroom. It seems curious, given the close attention paid to these matters, that five of the jury of twelve that was then empanelled should have been licensed victuallers, a group with which Jabez had had his troubles over the years; while the judge, Mr Gainsford Bruce, was a former Conservative MP, though one who liked to describe himself as 'progressive', who had sat in the Commons with Jabez.

Jabez's counsel, O'Connor, asked at the outset that most of the charges against Balfour be struck from the record, on the grounds that they had not been specified in the warrant for extradition. Mr Justice Bruce refused him. The charges involving all the defendants were then read out: making false entries, publishing false accounts, circulating false balance sheets and in Jabez's case, obtaining £20,000 by false pretences in the affair of Octavius Greig, and converting to his own use the £1,500 from the American venture (the property deal with Lord Sudeley in Wichita, Kansas).

The Attorney-General then rose to present his case. Sir Richard Webster, Jabez noted in *My Prison Life*, was hard, but not unduly vindictive or discourteous. Some nine months older than Jabez, he had prospered early both at the bar and in politics: Queen's Counsel at thirty-five, Attorney-General – an office he would hold three times – at forty-two, with a seat found for him at Conservative Launceston. 'It is unlikely', records his entry in the *Dictionary of National Biography*, 'that in 32 years in the bar [until 1895 he maintained his private practice even while Attorney-General] any man ever had more work to do, or earned more money.'

Sir Richard's core indictment was this: 'Transactions in tens of thousands, almost in millions, took place by the interchange of cheques between these various companies, sometimes and almost without exception, scarcely a penny passing, whereby profits to the extent of tens of thousands were supposed to be earned, sometimes by one company and sometimes by another, and arising out of these sham bogus transactions, which consisted in nothing but one clerk drawing out a cheque in the name of one company and paying it into the account of the other, and that second company drawing a cheque sometimes for exactly the same amount and handing it back again. On the basis of faith generated by these transactions, poor unfortunate people were induced to subscribe their money, it passing into this vast sink never to come out again.'

The detail was huge and tedious. The Official Receiver Wheeler was on the stand for seven days. On day three, there were gloomy forecasts that the case might run until Christmas. On day five, Brock's counsel Edward Marshall Hall, who would later become the most celebrated advocate in the land, invited the judge to rule that all the defendants bar Balfour should be discharged, on the grounds that a man could not be accused of a crime in connection with a subject on which he had already been judicially examined, as had happened during the liquidation proceedings. Balfour, too, had been examined in this way, Hall conceded, but his trip to Argentina debarred him from making this plea. The judge was unmoved.

O'Connor's arm-waving interventions were already trying the patience of both the judge and his fellow counsel. 'We shall adjourn now,' said Bruce wearily at the end of a day punctuated by O'Connor's confusions. 'I shall take care to revise my brief as much as possible,' O'Connor assured him. 'I am sure you will,' acknowledged the judge with a sigh one can almost hear even today.

The jury was restive too, though attentive enough to recognize the significance of testimony given on day eleven that Dibley had repeatedly warned Balfour to regulate the loans and advances paid to directors. By the end of that day's proceedings, some of the jurymen had become almost mutinous, arguing that the trial was keeping them away from their businesses and they wanted compensation. This request was refused, though the judge promised to grant them some exemption from future jury service.

The numbers in court had declined during Wheeler's seven days on the stand but picked up again as O'Connor began to present the case for Jabez. On day fourteen he apologized to the court, and indeed to the country, for the 'stupendous folly' of his client's disappearance to Argentina. But he also complained of the 'persecution' to which Jabez had been subjected, especially by the press. The press, he maintained, had driven Balfour out of the country (laughter). It had even attacked the characters of honourable women, particularly one who had recognized the accused as her guardian, and who had exhibited the finest traits of feminine nature – fidelity to a man in trouble – by going into exile with her benefactor. Here at last Jabez's composure broke, and he wept.

O'Connor was succeeded by Marshall Hall, making the case for Brock in what his biographer Edward Marjoribanks rated as one of his greatest performances. Then came Mr Woodfall, blaming everyone else for Dibley's predicament to a point where other counsel protested – and tellingly asking why Dawson Burns, whose lieutenant Dibley had been, was not facing charges too. By the rules of those days, none of those arraigned gave evidence, and only Mr Atherley-Jones, for Theobald, called witnesses.

The courtroom was as packed as it had been at the beginning of the trial when the Attorney-General rose on the afternoon of day sixteen to make his final, notably unshowy, appeal to the jury. Then at last it was time for Mr Justice Bruce to sum up. He took three hours – a briefer performance than most in the court had expected. The jury retired. Jabez, looking relaxed, helped himself to a cup of tea and read the evening papers. Brock, the beneficiary of Marshall Hall's matchless expertise, also looked cheerful, laughing and making jokes, but Dibley and Morell Theobald seemed subdued. Major Wright was still absent through illness.

After a little more than two hours the jury returned. For Balfour, Brock and Theobald the verdict was 'guilty'. On Dibley, the jurors had failed to agree and were never, in the view of the foreman, likely to do so. Sentences were deferred until a second trial before a fresh jury had dealt with the charges against Balfour alone in the case of Whitehall Court, the fish farmer Greig, and the missing £20,000. The case involving the American venture was dropped for lack of evidence.

The testimony of Jabez's nephew Leonard Balfour Burns on day three must have extinguished any lingering hope that he might avoid conviction. Next day O'Connor asked the judge's permission for Jabez to make a statement. Mr Justice Bruce registered no objection, and now for the first time in the proceedings, the voice of Jabez Spencer Balfour was heard in the court.

Some found his statement – denying that he had received anything more than the share of the proceeds that had been agreed in the Whitehall Court deal – long and meandering. Others, like the special correspondent of the *Croydon Advertiser*, thought it a *tour de force*, displaying all his old mastery. 'Balfour's composure and alertness were simply amazing, and judge, counsel, jury and spectators listened with new and revived interest to the details of the case in the nimble hands of the defendant … The statement was distinguished by all the characteristic cleverness of the man.'

But his cleverness could not save him now. The jury was out for only thirty-five minutes. The case might have been wrapped up immediately, but the judge – cruelly, Jabez later complained – ruled that sentencing should be deferred to the following day.

On Thursday, 28 November, still more were crammed into the courtroom, and more turned away, than on any previous day. Even the clerk of the court found himself sharing his seat. The judge was half an hour late. He began by striking out all remaining charges on the indictment, including those against Dibley and Major Wright, for whom the ordeal was over. Pleas in mitigation were made, and character witnesses called to attest the high reputation of Morell Theobald – which the judge, from his own knowledge, endorsed – and the mental and physical stress he was suffering. Theobald's sentence was four months' imprisonment; Brock's, nine months. Brock, said the judge, was deserving of sympathy, but even so, should have known better. These two, Bruce accepted, had been no more than bit players, working to Jabez's script.

When he turned to Jabez, his tone became colder and sterner. Jabez Balfour, he said, had been convicted on two indictments of offences of great gravity, involving frauds in the management of public companies. He had carried out with great deliberation a long and extensive series of frauds. He had been the chief actor: others had succumbed to his pressure to assist him, but he was the master mind. A sentence of great severity was required. It was painful to have to impose such a punishment on a man of high ability, but justice and the reputation of a great trading nation demanded it. It was true, the judge conceded, that had Jabez's schemes come to fruition his projects might have turned out successfully, since the fraud might then never have come to light; but success could not turn fraud into honesty.

And then came a peroration which indicated that the sentence he meant to impose reflected rather less the charges brought to the court than the grievous injuries Jabez had inflicted on those who had put their trust in him. 'It is the duty of those who administer the law,' the judge said, 'to prove that the man of position who transgresses it must undergo the same punishment as the common thief. I am sure that no small part of your punishment is the remorse you must feel at having darkened many a humble home. No prison doors can shut out from your ears the cry of the widow and the orphan whom you have ruined.' The sentence was to be seven years' imprisonment with hard labour on each of the two counts in the first indictment, to run concurrently; and the same on the second indictment, making fourteen years in confinement in all.

Though he must have known that a long term in prison awaited him, Jabez could not have expected a sentence which would lock him away for so long. During the final stages of the trial he had obsessively doodled an enormous number eight on his notepad, indicating no doubt that an eight-year term was what he expected. And here was a sentence of almost twice that duration. But he did not intend the world to see his dismay. As the sentence was delivered, O'Connor rushed from the court as if overwhelmed by emotion, but when he returned he bounded into the waiting room with sandwiches and champagne. 'He would not allow me to speak to him,' Jabez recalled in his memoirs, 'until I had made one of the most tremendous, mixed and indigestible luncheons in my life.' He would not have been aware that while this feast was in progress, two women, whose identities pressmen failed to establish, had asked to see him, only to be told that they could not do so. One wept as officials turned them away.

What Jabez truly felt now that the game was up he recorded a decade later in *My Prison Life*. 'Ordinary words cannot describe the feelings of a man in my position. It seemed then the end of everything. One's whole life flashes across one's brain in a second – childhood, youth, earliest ambition, family life, children, success, failure, ruin – and fourteen years' penal servitude. The sentence was so colossal that I quite failed to realize it, and at one moment my brain seemed to regard it as one enormous joke.'

He was taken, past newspaper placards proclaiming 'Heavy Sentence on Balfour', to Holloway prison. For a while he remained there in a kind of judicial limbo awaiting further proceedings against him, but when on 9 December he was taken by black Maria to Newgate, the Crown declined to proceed with the case. He remained three days more in Holloway. Then on 12 December he was given the prison number V460 and removed to Wormwood Scrubs for the start of his prison life proper.

From the moment he was returned from the court to Holloway, Jabez's access to newspapers ceased. Therefore he would not have seen immediately after his conviction the reports of the death of yet another Liberator victim, a man called Follinfant, from Cable Street, Tower Hamlets, discovered dead in Greenwich Park. A card was found in the man's pocket, which read: 'My love, my only love, Emma; Charley, pride of my heart; never put your money in public companies. It was your father's downfall. Look to your mother.'

Part Three

Yours faithfully, A.J. Balfour

14

Prisoner V460

We bless thee for the friends we miss
  Who made our peace, and stilled our pain
We trust thee on some height of bliss
  To bring us close to them again.

John White Chadwick (1840–1904)

The England into which Jabez Balfour emerged at the end of his jail sentence on 14 April 1906 was a drastically different place from the country that had despatched him to prison more than ten years earlier. Many of the great cornerstones of the 1890s were gone. Gladstone, his party leader throughout his years in Parliament, had died in May 1898, seven months short of his ninetieth birthday: 300,000 people came to the lying-in-state in Westminster Hall. The Queen, who could not stand him, outlasted him by less than three years. Lord Salisbury, the most formidable Conservative of the age, who had left the premiership in the summer of 1902 to be succeeded by Jabez's namesake and *bête noire*, Arthur Balfour, had also died while Jabez was in Parkhurst. So had George Dibley, who had stood trial beside him, though the severely ailing Morell Theobald lasted until 1908. George Brock died the following year.

The Hotel Cecil, rescued and given that name by the ingenuity of the Official Receiver, had successfully opened its doors and become one of the most admired hotels in Europe. Hyde Park Court had survived, though with substantial damage caused by a fire that broke out in one of its lift shafts in April 1898. Britain had been at war: in the Egyptian Sudan, where Kitchener had triumphed at Khartoum and Omdurman, and then with the Boers in South Africa. The United States had seen its great gold rush and lost a president – William McKinley – to a gunshot from an anarchist. In Russia, in 1905, some 200,000 people had marched on the Tsar's winter palace; the palace guards had fired on the crowd, killing 500 people, an event which provoked the first, failed, revolution.

In Britain a new generation of Liberal leaders, far more to Jabez's radical tastes than the stubbornly unradical Rosebery, had emerged with the arrival at the head of the party of Henry Campbell-Bannerman, who earmarked Asquith for the Treasury and David Lloyd George for the Board of Trade. During Jabez's last days in jail the Liberals called an election, in which they won 400 seats; but thirty MPs were elected for the new Labour party, which had effectively come into existence only six years before. Even as the Liberals celebrated a landslide victory, the 'Strange Death of Liberal England' was on the horizon.

While Jabez sat sewing his mailbags, taking his notes, and handing out books and useful advice to his fellow prisoners, Thomas Hardy had published *Jude the Obscure*, Joseph Conrad had written *Lord Jim* and H. G. Wells *The War of the Worlds*;

George Bernard Shaw had brought audiences flocking to Man and Superman and Major Barbara; Elgar had finished The Dream of Gerontius; and Sigmund Freud The Interpretation of Dreams. Samuel Butler, whose name Jabez had purloined in his fugitive years, had written The Way of All Flesh, though it did not appear until 1902.

Some of Jabez's favourite causes had prospered in his absence. The lot of working people had been alleviated by legislation such as the Compensation for Accidents to Workmen Act, though the House of Lords had ruled in the Taff Vale case that unions could be sued by employers for the actions of their agents, which severely restricted the scope for industrial action. There was still no prospect of legislation allowing women to vote in parliamentary elections, though the suffragette movement was on the march by the time of Jabez's release. The drudgery of the housewife (or that of the house-maid, in those middle-class homes which could afford to employ them) was beginning to be alleviated by inventions such as the vacuum cleaner.

But it was the revolutionary developments in science and technology that were transforming everyday life. E. F. Benson, who lived through those years, wrote in his classic memoir, As We Were: 'These years saw, glimmering from the darkness of the unknown, such manifestations of scientific marvels that no other short period can point to. Motor cars and moving pictures, telephones and electric lighting, X-rays and other ultra-spectrum potencies, flying and submarines and the begin-nings of wireless were all then in process of discovery and adaptation to human uses. Nowadays [he was writing in 1930] these have passed into the categories of conveniences which we take for granted, but then they were amazing and scarcely credible.'

The changes that must have astonished Jabez most as he emerged from prison at the end of his sentence were the new means of rapid communication, the developing use of electricity, and above all the motor car. In 1898 a message sent by the system that Signor Marconi had first demonstrated in 1895 was reported to have travelled from Wimereux near Boulogne to the South Foreland in Kent at a dizzying fifteen words per minute. By 1901 Marconi was using it to send messages across the Atlantic. Electricity, something of a rich man's toy when Jabez installed it at Burcot, was still too expensive for most households, but in public enterprises its use was steadily growing. Most over-ground railways might be sticking to steam, but the London Underground – its passenger count rising from 165 million a year in 1896 to 331 million twelve years later – ran on electricity. Electric trams were filching custom from horse-drawn buses. And increasingly weaving amongst them, bringing apprehension and fear to pedestrians, was the motor car.

The motor car caught on much more slowly in Britain than in Germany or across the Atlantic, partly because these new-fangled inventions were so expensive but also because the restrictions placed on them were so severe. The maximum speed allowed for a motor car was initially 4 mph in the country and 2 mph in town, and the driver had to arrange for a man with a warning flag to precede it. Under pressure from manufacturers, the Conservative government sought to ease these restrictions in subsequent legislation, raising the speed limit to 12 mph and then proposing to scrap it while introducing a requirement to register cars, to equip them with number plates and impose stiffer penalties for reckless or dangerous driving. But the Commons rebelled and insisted that the new top limit should be 20 mph.

Yet even for those who had observed its development, the motor car remained a creature of alien menace. In 1905, introducing a bill to further increase available penalties, the Liberal member for Barnstaple, Mr Soares, said his bill reflected the wide prevalence of irritation and annoyance caused by almost all motor cars to the rest of the public by reason of the smell, smoke and dust they produced, and the deep indignation and alarm at the dangers to which the more reckless drivers exposed both pedestrians and persons riding and driving horses. For someone like Jabez, who for more than ten years had been shielded by prison walls from such experiences, the sight of a motor car must have been still more intimidating.

Little of this had penetrated the grim confining walls of his various prisons – Holloway, Wormwood Scrubs, Pentonville, Portland and Parkhurst – during Jabez's long incarceration. The first he knew of Queen Victoria's death was when 'king' replaced 'queen' in the order of service at morning worship. The newspapers he had always read so thirstily were denied to him. Visits were few and mostly restricted to twenty minutes. In the early years of his sentence he was permitted to write only three letters a year – though by the end of his term his good behaviour had gained him the privilege of one a month. Each letter written permitted one reply in return.

No doubt, though he does not say so in his prison memoirs, special provision would have been made to inform him of events which closely affected him: the death in March 1897 of his alienated sister Cecil, wife of the Revd Dawson Burns and mother of Leonard Balfour Burns, whose testimony had done so much to ensure her brother's conviction. His surviving brother James (John, with whom he had fallen out so painfully over his employment at Hockley Hall, had died in February 1894, while Jabez was in Argentina) was more forgiving. In *My Prison Life* Jabez records a visit from James in Pentonville. Though their tastes and pursuits were different, they had always been close, and the affection James bore him had not been diminished, but rather increased, by his ruin. The encounter, even so, left him drained and ill: within hours he was running a fever and there followed one of the two most serious illnesses of his life.

Not only was Jabez cut off from the world; he was also, in a sense, cut off from himself. In the nine years that followed his arrival at Wormwood Scrubs he never saw himself in a mirror, and when he finally did he could not recognize the old man that he saw before him. 'I shall never forget the shock. I started from it with affright, for I can honestly affirm that I did not recognize a single feature of the face that I beheld reflected in it. It was that of a perfect stranger...I learnt then for the first time the full and sorrowful significance of the tears which I had seen in the eyes of the two or three relatives and dear friends who had visited me in my bonds.' A *Daily Mail* reporter, who interviewed him on his release, described the once portly confident and swaggering Jabez as 'a little old gentleman, with a delicate face, not pallid, but sunburnt, and the nervous, curious manner of one who is watched'.

His prison life proper had begun at the Scrubs. A convict barber was sent in to shave him, which he had expected since he knew that beards were not permitted in prison, and then to close-crop his hair, which he had not. When he put his hand to his head halfway through the operation he found it almost as smooth as a billiard ball. Next, in a process that powerfully signalled his degradation, he was ordered to shed the conventional dress he had been permitted at Holloway and exchange it for prison uniform, complete with a cap which announced both his prisoner number and the length of his sentence: V460-14.

His cell, unlike some of those he would later inhabit, was clean and roomy, and because of his age and apprehension over his health he was permitted a mattress instead of the standard bare boards. Here he settled down that first night to calculate how many days and nights would elapse before he was free. Allowing for the remission for good conduct he was determined to earn, the answer, he decided was 3,833 days – to 20 May 1906, his expected date for release, in his sixty-third year.

In those days, all prisoners began their sentences in a local prison such as the Scrubs for a breaking-in period which usually lasted six to nine months. Jabez was at the Scrubs for just short of seven, held in confinement for twenty-three hours a day, and employed in sewing mailbags. But on 4 June, the following summer, this 'silent and solitary existence' was unexpectedly interrupted. He was handcuffed and put in a four-wheeler cab which, with unintentional cruelty, carried him past his old grand home at Marlborough Gate to Waterloo station on his way to a destination still unrevealed to him.

The billboards on the station, poignant reminders of what free men were engaged in, were celebrating the result of the Derby, won by a horse owned by the Prince of Wales. As the train passed through Raynes Park station he saw on the plat-form a friend from his days of freedom, awaiting his morning train into town. Was Jabez's train taking him towards Portland or Parkhurst? It proved to be the more agreeable option – Parkhurst, close to his mother's old home on the Isle of Wight. In his heyday Jabez had purchased a farmhouse on the edge of Parkhurst Forest: now he could see it from the prison exercise yard.

Five days later he was moved again. This time it was the destination he feared: Portland, a place with the grimmest of reputations. No need, he says in *My Prison Life*, to inscribe over the gateway the legend 'Abandon hope, all ye who enter here', since the massive grey walls said it so powerfully. Here, petty and gratuitous tyranny flourished, often applied by warders who themselves were victims of bullying by their superiors. Jabez was once reproved for smiling at a fellow prisoner, and twice for looking up at the sky. With its huge fortifications, its civil guards stationed at vantage points, its proximity to a military barracks ready to fire on fugitives, the whole place seemed designed to impress upon its inhabitants that they had no chance of escape. Jabez would later call Portland 'a heart-breaking, soul-enslaving, brain-destroying hell upon earth'.

On 26 August 1896, nine months into his sentence, he was told that his time of segregation was over. That sounded like an improvement, but in many ways it was not. Despite the rule that 'star' prisoners – in effect, first-time offenders – should be kept away from old lags, he now found himself in the company of hardened and brutal criminals. He was moved from a decent cell to a 'box', as he called it, 7 feet high, 7 feet long and 4 feet wide, separated from the cell next door only by strips of corrugated iron, so that every sound from his neighbours was immediately audible. His stitching of mailbags resumed, interrupted by a spell in the prison hospital when the doctor was worried that Jabez was losing weight. Later they found him work with the shoemakers – 'we had one or two dynamiters, kindly and well-behaved men;...one or two doctors, an accountant, a bank manager, two or three solicitors, a sailor, a soldier, one or two tradesmen, one or two murderers, and one or two clerks who had got into trouble through backing horses'. Later still he was moved to the tinsmith's shop.

Then, in the peremptory fashion which for him was the mark of prison regimes, he was told one Sunday that he would be going to London the next morning. Again the train up to Waterloo; again the news billboards hinting at pursuits of happier days (this time, the England cricket team's results in Australia); and again the route past familiar addresses – his Hotel Cecil, his old home in Whitehall Court. The purpose of this visit was the compilation of a statement for his examination in bankruptcy, a process he found hardly less demeaning than prison, partly because of the autocratic manner of those who questioned him, but partly too because he was now forced to confront the claims – most of them, in his judgement, bogus – made against him.

To find himself in Pentonville after Portland was like a kind of reprieve. There was none of Portland's brutality. 'Grim as the place is,' he wrote in *My Prison Life*, 'I shall always associate it with the humanity and patience which I found there.' He stayed much longer than anyone had expected, because the lack of exercise, the dirt of the prison, the strain of having to deal with the bankruptcy case, and the painful reunion with his brother combined to make him ill enough for a transfer to the infirmary, where his state swiftly grew worse. He remained very ill – 'closely and apprehensively watched' – for much of December, and though allowed up for a while on Boxing Day 1896 he was not considered fit to go back to the bankruptcy court until the following April.

In a way the illness had been a blessing, removing him from Portland for much of the winter and persuading the prison authorities that he could not be allowed to return there because of his precarious health. This time, having finished at last with the bankruptcy court, he was told he would be going back over the Solent to Parkhurst.

He arrived there on 27 April 1897, and found his reacquaintance with the Isle of Wight nothing short of inspiring. At first the jobs he was given to do – needlework (he made an indifferent seamstress, he says), working in the printing shop for a malevolent master printer, an orderly in the stores – were tedious and depressing, but a spell dispensing books in the prison library was much more to his taste. He could make himself useful now writing letters for fellow prisoners, discreet and decent expressions of love included; learning Spanish, and teaching some French to a fellow prisoner; writing petitions for those with a grievance but lacking the means to express it – though of all those he wrote, only one, for a one-legged, one-armed lifer called Thomas, produced the result he wanted.

He was also now in the care of an enlightened governor, who, when Jabez was twice reported for petty offences – wishing another prisoner a happy new year, illicitly possessing a piece of waste paper – declined to impose any penalty, thus ensuring that his claim to maximum remission remained in place and confirming his reputation, as Parkhurst warders told journalists after he was released, as a model prisoner.

Meanwhile the world moved on into a new century. In September 1903 Jabez celebrated, if that is the word, his sixtieth birthday. What might he have been at sixty, had life worked out as he'd planned? An honoured and envied businessman, a government minister, perhaps with the words Rt Hon to preface his name ... But in time his mental count of days served became more encouraging: half his sentence completed; then two thirds; then, in October 1903, three quarters.

His final countdown to freedom began in May 1905, a year before the time he had calculated back in the Scrubs nearly ten years before as the target date for release, reckoning on maximum remission for good behaviour. He marked the progress of this final year out of the world with an almost child-like joy. First the privilege of being allotted the distinctive blue uniform which proclaimed that a prisoner had less than twelve months left to serve; the 'unutterable joy' on 4 September of his last prison birthday, his sixty-second; then his last prison Christmas, the happiest Christmas Day, he says, of his life; his last New Year's Day; his last Good Friday, with every sign now that release was imminent. His hair and his beard were allowed to grow; there were interviews, health checks, an assignment to be measured for clothes. All this, as he thought, for release in mid-May.

But there Jabez was wrong. He discovered, at the last moment as usual, that his day of freedom had been fixed for Saturday, 14 April 1906, the day that followed Good Friday. He had set himself as a farewell gift to the prison to catalogue its library, a task which he now had to work through the early hours of that final Saturday morning to complete. He finished in time for breakfast. What happened next, after 3,780 days, on his count, in confinement, deserves his own words:

> In a few minutes I heard footsteps on the landing. The door was opened, and an assistant warder said to me quite naturally: 'Balfour, you are wanted at the Governor's office. You are to bring your kit with you.' I obeyed mechanically. I should like to have shouted, screamed or danced. With a great effort I controlled

myself and tried to assume an air of composure. I reached the office, was directed to a small ante-room where all sorts of well-nigh forgotten articles – a white shirt, a white handkerchief, a necktie, braces, gloves and the like – were lying on a table. I handled them with difficulty. I fumbled so dreadfully that the good-natured assistant warder came to my help.

Then I appeared before the Governor. He was very kind, as he had always been to me. He told me that my son was waiting for me at the gate. He sent for him. We met and shook hands for the first time for over thirteen years. I thanked the Governor and bade him goodbye, and accompanied by my son, walked through the pleasant garden in front of the Governor's offices. A wicket in the great prison gate was opened for us. How I scrambled through it I cannot tell. There was quite a crowd of warders outside, returning from breakfast and waiting to enter on the duties of the day. When they saw me with my son, there was a sudden hum of surprise. I also honestly believe that it was a hum of pleasure. They fell back to let us pass. An open fly was waiting for us; my daughter-in-law was seated in it. We jumped into the fly. I hardly realized what had happened, or where I was, or what I said.

After about an hour's drive we left the fly, I was taken along a little pier to a little steamboat, and a few minutes afterwards I woke up to the consciousness that I was on another element, that I was crossing the sea.

Then I understood that the hills and woodlands we were so rapidly approaching were part of the mainland of my native country, and, more wondrous still, that I was FREE.

15

Balfour of the *Dispatch*

'Tis ne'er too late, while life shall last,
    A new life to begin.

E. S. Armitage (1841–1931)

The boat on which Jabez Spencer Balfour began his journey to his new life of freedom took him from Yarmouth to Lymington, from where he and his little party could ride up by train with no officious prison officers or policemen, no one to order that blinds be drawn to shut out the view of the countryside, and little chance now that this crushed and saddened old man would be recognized by gawpers and jeerers. They left the train at Basingstoke. Here Jabez was whisked away in a car which he inspected closely before climbing in for his first motor journey. And then, for most of the pressmen now urgently seeking him, he simply vanished. Only the *Daily Mail* caught up with him, and that was hardly surprising, since the car belonged to the *Mail's* proprietor. The *Mail* was another phenomenon of the new, changed world to emerge during his imprisonment, launched by Alfred Harmsworth, later Lord Northcliffe, in 1896. The car was there to take him away to a hideout where he would write his prison memoirs for serialization in the great press tycoon's *Weekly* (later, *Sunday*) *Dispatch*. 'For a time,' wrote one of Northcliffe's lieutenants, John Hammerton, 'Jabez was the apple of Northcliffe's eye. Very generous payment was made to him.'

The money mattered. Jabez emerged from prison virtually destitute. His children had been forced to pawn their belongings, and his series in the *Dispatch* would provide them all with bread and help him to recover himself. The car took him to a cottage near Maidenhead where he straightaway set to work, writing 20,000 words within seventy-two hours of leaving the prison. 'The words fell from him red hot' it was recorded. But he still found time to talk to the man from the *Mail*, whose job was to whet the public's appetites for the launch of the series on Sunday in the *Dispatch*.

'Four times have I seen Jabez Balfour,' the journalist wrote on 18 April. 'Once as J. Spencer Balfour, radiant and successful on a hot, sultry night when he entertained the House of Commons to a brilliant, convincing and epigrammatic speech ("our future postmaster general" as a Liberal colleague described him); next, as Jabez Balfour, standing, in a hushed court, to receive, apparently unmoved, his fourteen years' sentence; then, years after, a small birdlike figure, seen through a peephole, in the hideous costume of the broad arrow, scrubbing for dear life his cell at Portland; and today, when after a two days' search by motor, I found somewhere many miles from London, a small old gentleman at a table, surrounded by masses and masses of manuscripts and newspapers, a figure that, frankly, I should not have recognized anywhere.

'A tiny maiden of four was playing among the papers, and his son, who after an extensive parley at the door had admitted me and my camera, told me that her grandfather had seen her yesterday for the first time, and that he idolized her, a beautiful child with all the mental alertness and bright humour that seem to characterize the Balfour family.' Balfour willingly broke off from his writing. 'I cannot refuse the *Daily Mail*,' he may or may not have said.

What he wrote in those days would enthral and appal middle-class England for months, the lead on page one of the *Weekly Dispatch* for twenty-six weeks before being displaced by reports of a horrible rail crash near Grantham. The first instalment appeared on 22 April, just eight days after his release. 'What a sensation the publication of his prison experiences in the *Sunday Dispatch* created!' wrote the veteran journalist Bernard Falk, later himself editor of the *Dispatch*, in his memoirs *He Laughed in Fleet Street*. Falk worked at this time for the *Evening News*, also a Northcliffe paper, but unlike the *Mail*, the *News* had not been let into the secret of Jabez's whereabouts. 'After an extended acquaintance with Sunday paper features, I am persuaded that none ever created a sensation comparable with that provoked by Jabez Balfour's prison reminiscences . . . in respect to the excitement they were to create, his reminiscences were never to be approached by any other notable Sunday paper feature, not excluding the story of John Lee, the Babbacombe murderer they could not hang, the spiritualistic revelations of the Rev Vale Owen, the serial publication of *All Quiet on the Western Front*, and the prison memoirs of Horatio Bottomley.'

The pieces were titled 'From a Living Tomb, by Jabez Spencer Balfour': Spencer for respectability, Jabez for recognition. The luridness of their presentation owed at least as much to the cartoons that adorned them, mostly by George P. Carruthers, as to Jabez's text. Here were grotesques: a 'convict Caliban', with a drawing by Carruthers designed to put readers of the *Dispatch* off their food for a week. '"Pick that up:"' read the caption. 'A warder cowing into obedience a giant negro convict, who Mr Jabez Balfour describes as the most repulsive prisoner he ever met.' Here too were an imprisoned anarchist who went 'raving mad', and 'a Negro convict [this time the cartoon is unsigned, but very much school of Carruthers] sentenced to penal servitude for life for murder, overwhelmed with terror at a mouse which had made an unexpected appearance in his cell'.

Jabez subscribed, Carruthers still more so perhaps, to the then prevalent view that the criminal classes looked different from ordinary people. But ordinary people – even the sort of people who took the *Weekly Dispatch* – were there too in profusion, reminding readers that even the respectable folk next door might qualify one day for Portland or Parkhurst. Jabez had met a host of professional men in his confinement and had noted down their behaviour as assiduously as that of habitual criminals. Lawyers, he said, made the best prisoners, doctors the worst, though he also – and here he hoped he did not sound prejudiced – found that the most difficult prisoners to manage, 'the most violent, aggressive, cunning and ungrateful', were the Jewish ones. Germans, however, he singled out for praise.

Somehow they always seemed to turn their time in prison to good use, treating it as a preparation for their return to law-abiding lives once released. 'A very clever German convict once confided to me: "I shall stop in England. After all, it is better than Germany, for there is no compulsory military service and much less official bullying. I can lie in bed and smoke on your Sundays, which are hateful. So when my young brother Karl comes over I shall tell him that his best way of learning English is to go in as I have done for a three years' 'lagging'!"'

The world of horror and terror and degradation evoked by Carruthers clearly suited the requirements of Northcliffe more than Jabez's own agenda. His was a much more sombre objective: to describe prison life as seen from the inside, by a man whose background, education and station in life would normally have kept him well clear of it. Others who had suffered similar fates to his own, he explained, had written about their prison experience largely in terms of their own deprivation and sufferings: he hoped as far as he could to steer clear of that theme. As, for the most part, he did, though complaining from time to time at the injustice he felt he had suffered, at the wrecking of his attempts to save his stricken companies, of slights shown to him by authorities in and out of his prisons. At one point he even claimed that his side of the Liberator story had never been told. His series in the *Dispatch*, and its subsequent, staider version in his book *My Prison Life*, are surprisingly free from such self-exculpation. They are far more concerned with the failure of the system either to deter or to reform.

Jabez had kept notes whenever he was allowed to. That practice was banned in the early days of his sentence and banned again by a newly installed governor during his time at Parkhurst. This was the one occasion during his sentence when Jabez petitioned the home secretary on his own behalf rather than for others. Two of the world's noblest books, *Don Quixote* and *The Pilgrim's Progress*, he argued, had been written in jail with the access to pen and ink now denied to him. It made no difference. The ban stayed in place.

Before his notebook had been confiscated he had occasionally noted down the sufferings of especially vulnerable prisoners, especially those with delirium tremens now they were no longer able to drink. But even the routine treatment of prisoners sometimes inflicted what in his view amounted to suffering. He protested, on his fellow inmates' behalf as well as his own, at the constant searches, both of bodies and cells, which he calculated he must have undergone some 13,000 times in his 3,780 days of imprisonment. Here Carruthers had augmented Jabez's outraged prose with a picture of a warder 'looking for traces of tobacco in the mouth of a stark naked convict'. Worst of all was the practice known as 'dry baths', in which prisoners were made to strip naked and their bodies and clothes were thoroughly searched: the most degrading, he said, of all prison practices. He condemned the prison food – the diet as much as the way the food was prepared and delivered – particularly for its inadequacy. Troubled by indigestion, he himself ate little and was shocked by the way that hungry fellow prisoners begged him for what he had left.

He railed, too, against the conspicuous favouritism shown to some prisoners, especially those with useful connections. There was in Parkhurst a man whose long sentence was mainly passed in the infirmary: a man of imposing appearance, stout, florid, and apparently the picture of health. He was treated with such indulgence that his fellow prisoners called him The King of Parkhurst, or My Lord. The staff resented him too. '— is reputed', Jabez wrote with uncharacteristic bitterness, 'to have been on something like friendly terms at the time of his conviction with a cabinet minister since deceased. This, from —'s former position in life, is by no means improbable, and the idea is current that he owes his extraordinary indulgence to this happy circumstance.'

Other aspects of prison life he found unpalatable but defensible. He described the appalling tension, in his own case inducing nausea, which gripped the prison when a sentence of flogging or birching was carried out. Yet he could not see any way, given the evil nature of some men confined in these places, that such apparently barbarous treatment could be avoided. Carruthers here provided a picture captioned 'a convict being whipped'. Other well-intentioned procedures, such as the segregation of the so-called 'star' prisoners from the old lags, were simply not carried out: in practice, first offenders were usually subjected to their foul ways and filthy language.

And what was the purpose of all the heavy secrecy which denied a prisoner information even about the detail of plans for release? Jabez had sometimes learned of impending changes, such as his journey to Holloway, not from prison officials but from fellow prisoners who were well enough in with warders to be fed such information. Worst of all was the treatment of foreign prisoners, who might have little English or none; very little was ever done for them in the way of interpretation. Jabez described the appalling decline of one young and engaging Italian prisoner serving a life sentence, with whom he used to converse in his own limited Italian. Occasionally a letter would arrive from the man's mother in Italy, but there was no one to read them to him. In his isolation, he fell into moral and mental decay, attacked a fellow prisoner, and was carted away to Broadmoor.

What purpose did it serve to make Sundays so boring? And why did religious services need to be so rushed, like some kind of 'devotional steeplechase'? And why did prison libraries – about the only consistent good influence in a prisoner's life – need to be subject to so many restrictions and be so meanly and wretchedly stocked?

The morals he drew from his prison experiences are summarized at the end of *My Prison Life*. Perhaps the most urgent was the need to correct the gross inequity of the sentences imposed by different judges – 'an inequality which it is hard, I will even say impossible, to reconcile with our habitual notions of the sanctity and righteousness of the administration of justice in this country'. Keen observers, he wrote, could predict when they heard the name of the judge who was trying the case what sentence was likely to follow. He quoted a string of examples from the men he met while in prison. In the tinsmith's shop at Portland, for instance, he had worked with two prisoners: one a respectable, quiet middle-aged man serving ten years, the other a young man of plausible address, well-spoken and fairly well educated, who was serving three. The man who was doing ten years had been convicted of an embezzlement where the sum involved was £72; the younger man, with his three-year term, of stabbing a girl to death in a brothel. In line with his resolution to evoke his own fate as little as possible, Jabez has nothing to say on his own account, but he must have reflected, during those long nights and days, on the disparity between the fate of, say, Hobbs at the hands of Hanging Hawkins and Brock before the more merciful Bruce.

His second prescription was a complete separation of first-time prisoners from chronic offenders, a principle honoured in theory but less so in practice. The only way to ensure effective segregation would be to have two classes of prison to fit these two classes of prisoner. And a third, more surprising perhaps, was his conclusion that for some of the hardest offenders the only practical course would be exile to somewhere like St Helena. 'Perpetual exclusion' is his term for it, and he took some comfort from the fact that General William Booth, 'the venerable head of the Salvation Army', had recently come to the same conclusion.

The response to Jabez's serial as the *Dispatch* pumped it out week by week delighted Northcliffe, who found him room in an office in his London headquarters Carmelite House, just off Fleet Street. Here he not only wrote his weekly pieces but dealt with the flood of letters they brought in. Keeping up with the correspondence, he confided to readers, was becoming harder than writing the series.

As September turned to October, interest in 'From a Living Tomb' was fading, and the pieces were relegated to obscure inside pages. But now the novice journalist had been given a new assignment: this was 'Crimson Crimes: the stories of famous crimes and their perpetrators'. Inevitably, Jack the Ripper was one. 'Jack the Ripper – mystery of his final identity solved' the *Dispatch* proclaimed over Jabez's byline on 11 November. 'I myself', Jabez claimed, 'have conversed with a man living in Johannesburg who knew two men who knew Jack the Ripper.' So who was he? A royal prince? The artist Walter Sickert? Probably not. 'A short, stout man of dark complexion, 5ft or 5ft 2 inches high with mutton chop whiskers, of good education and talent...now living in a remote British colony.' But, infuriatingly, unnamed.

The last prison memoir appeared on 9 December 1906, taking a poor second place to the latest 'Crimson Crime': 'Stolen Gold – the most daringly executed raid ever planned'. A further crime appeared every week until 10 February, when the sequence abruptly ended, making way for a third series: 'Life in Parliament. How I fought and won my first election in Tamworth' by Jabez Spencer Balfour.

The election of 1880, he wrote, had proved to be a landmark in Britain's political history. 'The parliament of 1880, from its birth to its death in the autumn of 1885, pulsated with a new life, was stirred by dramatic incidents, and was the birthplace of the political forces and methods which dominate us today.' Beneath Jabez's closing account of his success at Tamworth there appeared the words 'to be continued', but no more appeared. It seemed the subject matter had failed to meet Northcliffe's requirements for drama. However, on 3 March it was reported that the memoirs to which the *Dispatch* had devoted such an extraordinary ration of space had now been published as My *Prison Life* by Chapman and Hall. 'On the morrow of the King's speech at the new Old Bailey, when his Majesty said that while it was well that crime should be punished, it was better that the criminal should be reformed, Mr Jabez Balfour's long promised book, My *Prison Life*, is published. The book is interesting in many ways, and it should serve the good purpose at which it aims.' A surprisingly lack-lustre advertisement, this, when Jabez had dedicated his book to 'the Right Honourable Lord Northcliffe, in recognition of his interest in prison reform and of the sympathy, encouragement and help he has accorded to the author'.

The days of Jabez the journalist, it appeared, were over. He was now sixty-three, but his energy, his restlessness, and perhaps above all his need for money, necessitated yet another new career. He set himself up in an office in Chancery Lane as a consultant mining engineer, despite his distinct lack of qualifications. Now and then old associates and friends from his City days or his time with Northcliffe would come across his diminished but determined figure in the streets around Fleet Street. Bernard Falk, who had hailed his prison memoirs so warmly, was one: 'A grey and timid man, who seemed desirous of escaping recognition, sometimes passed us by in Whitefriars Street, and I would turn to a companion and say: "There goes Jabez Balfour! Did ever one of God's creatures look more inoffensive?" If I were asked that question, I should most certainly answer: "no". Jabez Balfour had the expression of a man who would not harm a fly, let alone a human being.'

But most of his old associates were lost to him, and though he had the affection of his loyal, forgiving son James and the company of his daughter-in-law and his grandchildren, his daughter Clara was gone. Twice widowed within seven years, and left with three children, she had married again – this time, in 1898, to Robert Warren Henderson. Close to the date of Jabez's release from prison, she and her husband, with whom she had two more sons, had emigrated to Canada, where she seems at last to have found a happy and settled life. Still, Jabez had plenty to occupy him. His new employment involved a great deal of travelling: to Africa, Australia and New Zealand, but also to Latin America. The business seems to have prospered until the outbreak of war in 1914, when the travelling had to stop.

He used to be seen around this time sitting serenely on a bench by the pond on Clapham Common, close to the house in Nightingale Lane, between Clapham and Wandsworth Common, where he lived for a while after prison. 'Of recent years', the *Daily Mail* recalled when he died, 'he was a well known figure – though his actual identity was never guessed – on Clapham Common, where on sunny days he would sit on a seat and read the newspapers – a quiet, calm, mild-mannered old man, kind to the children playing about him. On Sunday he would go to chapel and sing. The collection plate never passed him unavailingly.'

And yet he had one more adventure left in him, of a kind which demonstrates the astonishing resilience that had helped him through the degradations of prison, when his spirit was constantly tested but never broken. In August 1915, just short of his seventy-second birthday, at the height of the war, the former denizen of the Portland tinsmith's shop left England again and set off for Burma, on his way to a tin mine at a place called Namtu, some 200 miles north-east of Mandalay and 1,000 miles from Rangoon.

What happened there was recounted by his son at the coroner's inquest eight months later. 'It was like this,' James said. 'He was sent out, and when he arrived he was told something would be found for him by the resident manager.'

The coroner: 'In connection with some mines?'
James Balfour: 'Yes, for a company called the Burma Mines, or the Burma Corporation. I believe they are the largest tin mines in the world. When he got there the resident manager was away on sick leave for a month or so. My father stayed there till he returned. It was extremely hot out there, but he could stand any amount of heat. He had never been in better health in his life. He used to tell us wonderful stories about the frightful heat. When the manager returned he said with his experience he was quite convinced that a man of my father's age could not stand the climate. To use the manager's own words, he said he did not wish to kill him there, but my father said he was willing to take the chance. The general manager said, however, that he would not.'

251

The manager's act of kindness may well have helped to kill him. Jabez returned from the Burmese heat to a bitter London winter. Restless as ever, he was still, at seventy-two, in search of useful employment. The railway ticket found in his pocket when he died on his train to Wales was for Landore, the nearest station to the mining village of Morriston, where he was due to begin a new job the following week.

For the moment, though, he was living quietly in London. And here the story takes what at first sight seems an astonishing turn. Jabez rented an apartment in a modest boarding house in Ladbroke Grove, less than two miles from his childhood homes in Maida Hill and Paddington. He was not, however, alone. He was living, according to his landlady, Miss Dix, with his wife. The couple, she said, appeared to be in comfortable circumstances, but kept to their rooms and did not mix with the other boarders. 'I had no idea what Mr Balfour's occupation had been,' she told the *Mail*, 'but from his appearance – he seemed old before his time – I imagined he had lived long in the East and had come to England for health reasons.' He used to write a lot in the morning and go for a stroll in the afternoon. She had no idea who he was. Mrs Balfour, she added, was working in a munitions factory.

It was now almost fifty years since Jabez had married Ellen at Reigate. Since 1880 she had lived in care, first at the Priory in Roehampton and then since February 1896, soon after Jabez's conviction, at Springfield House, Kempston, near Bedford. It is true that some psychiatric disorders lessen with time. But given that Ellen had been confined for so many years with dementia, for her to have recovered to this degree, and especially to have a job in munitions, sounds little short of miraculous.

And it does not square with some of the other evidence. At the inquest on his father, James Balfour testified that his mother had been an invalid for thirty years. He also said that his father had spent Christmas with him and his family. If Ellen, restored to health, had been reunited with Jabez, she would surely have been there too. There's a curious reference in the inquest evidence to the whereabouts of Jabez's wife on the day he died: she had gone, it was said, to visit her sister in Bedford. But everything else suggests that the woman who lived with Jabez in his final days was not Ellen. Perhaps it was some fresh acquaintance made in the ten years or so since he came out of prison. Or perhaps it was Miss Freeman.

And so to the bitterly cold morning of Wednesday, 23 February 1916, Jabez's dash to Paddington (with no time for breakfast) and the morning train out to Wales, and the gentlemen in the carriage who enjoyed his tales of Burma just as his family had, and Jabez's comfortable lapse into sleep, and the ticket collector's insistent hand on his shoulder, and the search for the doctor, and the shaking of heads at Newport; and at 277 Ladbroke Grove, the constable at the door asking for Mrs Balfour, and the news addressed to the landlady that Jabez was dead.

16

Jabez Spencer Balfour (1843–1916)

Our little systems have their day;
They have their day and cease to be.

Alfred Tennyson (1809–92)

So what should we make of him, this Jabez, this J. Spencer
Balfour, with his huge business talent and his phenomenal
losses, his piety and his pretty young mistress, his temperance
and his splendid hoard of champagne, his philanthropy and his
money-grabbing. His mother had said of her eager, garrulous
five-year-old: 'He will be either good or evil – there is nothing
negative about him'. Contemplating the ruin not just of his
companies but of thousands of decent, deserving people who
trusted him and paid such a heavy price for that trust, the world
as a whole must have judged him if not evil, then, certainly,
wicked.

His conviction and sentence were greeted with joy and gratitude. 'The great imposture', said *The Times* 'has collapsed with
satisfying completeness.' 'Balfour's conduct', said *The Economist*
'stands out in a particularly despicable light, from the fact that
it owed its success to his posturing as a philanthropist with
strong religious convictions, and as a politician whose one

desire in life was the regeneration of the masses. Himself a shining light of liberationism and temperance propaganda, he was cunning enough to secure the co-operation of men of mark in the pulpit and on the platform as co-directors, while throughout the length and breadth of the country non-conformist ministers were, no doubt quite innocently on their part, made the means of bringing vast amounts of money into the Balfourian net.'

'He was a financier among politicians, a politician among financiers, and a man of religion among both,' the *Westminster Gazette*'s exposé said of him. 'His religion and his philanthropy lent unction to his politics. His religion, his philanthropy and his politics gave sanction to his financial schemes. His eminence as a financier gave him weight as a politician, solidity as a philanthropist, consideration as a man of religion.'

'Nor it is astonishing,' said the *Pall Mall Gazette*, 'that the swindler should be ever active in the cause of religion. For him there is no more profitable investment. His name is writ large upon subscription-lists, and the devout, being often simple, eagerly support the enterprises of so worthy a citizen. No doubt Mr Jabez Balfour, where he sowed £1, reaped £10, and the practical was not his only reward. There is, indeed, no man so wicked but would rock his conscience to sleep if he can, and what is more consolatory to the wrong doer than the personal conviction that he is doing good.'

Despicable, posturing, cunning, swindler, hypocrite – there were many such indictments. And yet some of those people closer to the world in which he had operated – the City, the lawyers, even some in the press which had harassed and excoriated him – were more understanding. Yes, he did wrong, they agreed; but most of all he was simply unlucky. Unlucky because what he did was what many others were doing, most of whom went to their graves admired as pillars of English society, as he would have been had recession not wrecked him. Nothing succeeds like success. Because they *looked* successful, they were destined to *be* successful. 'The world of London generally knows what it is about,' Mr Broune tells Lady Carbury in Trollope's *The Way We Live Now*, published in 1875 when the Liberator was on its way to becoming the nation's biggest and most successful building society. 'And the London world believes Mr Melmotte to be sound. I don't say that he has never done anything that he ought not to…But he is a man of wealth, power and genius.' These are Victorian values; though not quite the Victorian values lauded by Margaret Thatcher. For those who looked at the world in that way, Jabez in the final analysis was less swindling scoundrel than luckless scapegoat.

The great advocate Edward Marshall Hall (though he had a weakness for rogues, as he demonstrated in his friendship with Horatio Bottomley) sympathized with that view. In his *Famous Trials of Marshall Hall*, Hall's friend and biographer Edward Marjoribanks said that Hall took a lenient view of Jabez. 'In time, with the enormous increase in values, things might have come round, and, if Jabez's capital had come from big business instead of from the savings of the poor, it is just possible that he would not have had to resort to those ingenious devices to pay dividends, in order to keep his shareholders quiet, which brought him to ruin.'

'This was a man I neither liked nor trusted,' wrote Robert Farquharson, a Scottish Liberal MP, in his memoir *The House of Commons From Within*, 'and I used to call him "the animated Bath chap" from his resemblance to those dried pigs' faces which glare or grin at you from behind the plate glass of Italian warehouses, and I always used to remonstrate the whips for giving him the chance of good seats over the heads of better men. Like too many of his class, he concealed his sharp prac-tices behind the cloak of religion, but I doubt if, at all events at first, he was activated by the desire to break the eighth commandment. [Thou shalt not steal.] For it was only after his schemes began to go wrong that his error began, like the idle apprentice who puts his fingers in the till to pay his gambling debts, and I believe that some of his speculations on coming to maturity have done quite well.'

The company promoter H. Osborne O'Hagan, who had worked with Jabez on the Croydon tramway development, thought the depth of public feeling against him had made a fair trial impossible. Compared with others he'd had to work with, Balfour was upright and straight. The journalist Arthur Spender, who, with the help of the Official Receiver Wheeler, had put together for the *Westminster Gazette* an indictment of Jabez every bit as devastating as anything said about him in court, was full of remorse when he heard of the sentence. 'To my dismay,' he wrote in his memoirs, *Life, Journalism and Politics*, 'the judge sentenced him to fourteen years' penal servitude. His offence was undoubted, and he had greatly aggravated it by the circumstances of his flight. But he was by no means a common thief; his companies were originally sound ones with good and genuine schemes; and his transactions, though fraudulent, were for the most part desperate flounderings in the hope of covering up temporary embarrassments due to trade conditions. Many ramps of later days in which the operators have not only not been found out but received high recognition have been vastly more criminal... It had never occurred to me that Balfour could get more than three years' penal servitude, and had I foreseen the end I would never have touched the case. The idea that I had contributed to this excess of justice lay heavily on my mind for many years, and I was not comforted when Lord Justice Vaughan Williams used to descant on the iniquity of this sentence and urge me to take it up as a warning against hunting criminals in newspapers.'

This sense that what Jabez had done was no worse – indeed, was more deserving of forgiveness – than the actions of many eminent City figures who had got clean away with their wrongdoing seems to have been quite general in the City. They took much the same view as the great Lord Macaulay, one of the writers whom Jabez most delighted to read. That there are ten thousand thieves in London, he once wrote, is a very melancholy fact. But, looked at from a different point of view, it is a reason for exultation. For what other city could maintain ten thousand thieves? St Kilda would not support a single pickpocket. 'Our world', the historian Andrew Roberts writes in his foreword to a biography of another conspicuous rogue, the railway king Robert Hudson, by Robert Beaumont, 'was made by rogues as much as by angels.'

There have always been commercial empires like Jabez's with no great regard for the rules, and there always will be – and nowadays, they operate on a vastly greater scale. It is striking how much of what has been written about the spectacular collapses of WorldCom and Enron could have applied to Jabez.

Mr Ebbers was a one-off – an inveterate deal-maker, Baptist do-gooder and show-off. His shareholders loved him. His almost evangelical belief in his business grabbed people's attention...he collected assets the way other people collect stamps. (*Guardian*)

Those like Bernie Ebbers, founder of WorldCom...who couldn't face up to the harsh reality of delivering profits below the exponential growth predicted by lickspittle analysts, became desperate for short-term fixes to eke out the pretence of success. If the numbers didn't add up, they made them up...Mr Ebbers' company...clocked up heavy losses while claiming to make profits. It was a con-trick from start to finish. (*Sunday Telegraph*)

What they are uncovering is a combination of accounting fiddles, deceit and outright criminality designed to inflate short-term share prices by vastly overstating profits, and maximize the value of stock options granted to executives. (*Guardian*)

The role of the auditors in Jabez's empire has a ring of today about it, too. Arthur Andersen in the matter of Enron is simply the latest and most spectacular case (following Robert Maxwell, BCCI, Polly Peck) of auditors far too cosy with those they are there to police. Nothing, it seems, erodes the complacency in the City, which likes to treat such events as simply an uncharacteristic wobble, after which normal service will soon be resumed. But experience has proved the contrary. If there are any weak points in the dam, and there will be, greed and ingenuity, like the sea waters at Brading, will search them out and sooner or later find a way through.

Yet the most intriguing question with Jabez, as with other great rogues, conmen and fraudsters from Hudson through Horatio Bottomley to Robert Maxwell in our own day, is this: what did he see when he looked in the mirror? Did he see the respectable, pious, law-abiding figure he wanted people to believe in – or a hypocrite, a skilled commercial seducer and dissembler, a man whose public reputation was built on a massive fraud?

There seems to have been in Balfour – some contemporaries certainly detected it – just as there was in Maxwell, an excess of self-belief, which led him to say to himself: if I am doing these things, they must be all right. All right, in the sense that legal constraints I am breaking do not really matter; all right, in the sense that because I am who I am, I am going to succeed, I am going to get away with it. 'Any paper with my name to it will come right,' Trollope's Melmotte boasts shortly before his fall.

The writer Sheridan Morley observed of his friend Jeffrey Archer as they marched him away to prison: 'Everything he does, he thinks is going to be all right in the end.' Thus O'Hagan said of Jabez: 'His early success had given him such confidence in himself and his powers of raising money that he took risks which no careful financier would have done.'

Today it might even be judged that Jabez had symptoms of hypomania. The diagnostic tests used by the American Psychiatric Association for assessing mania or hypomania are these: grandiosity or exaggerated self-esteem, reduced need for sleep (Jabez slept for four hours a night), increased talkativeness, racing thoughts which ignore or sweep aside the views of other people, easy distractability, increased goal-directed activity in social or sexual life, work or school, and poor judgement exhibited in spending sprees, sexual adventures and foolish investments. Most of these descriptions fit Jabez to some degree. Some fit him perfectly.

In the final days before the crash, it would have been different: in the last few months of the Liberator, at the final annual meeting in the spring of 1892, when Jabez used its apparent success to inveigle unfortunate clients into making fresh investments which would bring them even greater ruin. It was then that Jabez, like Maxwell, moved from opportunistic malpractice into spectacular dishonesty.

Some, like the prosecution lawyers in the autumn of 1895, thought the whole of Jabez's enterprise from the founding of the Lands Allotment Company onwards had been designed for his own enrichment, and that the Liberator Building Society, whose apparent success made his name, was from the first simply an engine to fund the empire of which it was going to be part. Yet perhaps the two aspirations – the greater enrichment and glory of J. Spencer Balfour, and the welfare of thousands of people who had few resources and no kind of privilege – went together. That was the point, after all, about the original, biblical story of Jabez, and why it was particularly prized by pious non-conformists who were also intent on making their fortunes. Jabez asked God to enlarge his coast, and his coast was duly enlarged. Therefore, God must have approved and endorsed his ambition.

It is easy, now, to forget the sense of true independence the Liberator must have brought to families who, before Jabez appeared, could never have hoped to escape the clutches of the landlord, to have had a place of their own. The claim in the early days that the words 'No speculative builders need apply' could be written over the door of the Liberator seems in the light of the great speculative projects he entered into later to be the grossest hypocrisy. But was this progression from nurturing the hopes of the poor to offering profit-producing homes for the rich always intended? Even Arthur Spender, who studied his operations so closely, was not entirely sure that his motive had been greed all along. 'Into the depths of human motives, what sure plummet can be cast? In the complexities of human character, who shall judge or decide?'

There is much to admire in Jabez. He gave London some fine buildings, though not all of them have survived. Look across the Thames from the Waterloo side to the skyline of Whitehall Court on a winter night: few views in London have the same sense of fairy-tale fantasy. The Hotel Cecil – now gone – proved in its heyday to be just as magnificent as Jabez had planned and predicted. 'There was no more imposing room in London,' says *The Golden Age of British Hotels* by Derek Taylor and David Bush, 'than the Grand Ballroom which was over 100 feet long, 66 feet wide and a vast 46 feet high.' Similarly, by their pertinacity when everything seemed against them, Jabez and Henry Freeman gave Bembridge a fine harbour and the access it needed to bring in holiday trade, many acres of productive farming land and the ground which one day was to furnish an airfield.

His family, and most of all his much put-upon son James, who stood by him in such awful circumstances, seem to have been fond of him and he of them, as the Newport coroner noted after reading letters found in the dead man's pocket. He had lived in Argentina, in sin, as used to be said, with a younger woman not his wife, for whom he had acted as guardian after the death of her father. And yet his wife had been incurably ill for more than a decade; and this portly and unprepossessing man commanded the very real love and loyalty of the woman who lived with him, as she demonstrated in the way she fought for him. Even the business associates whom he misled and bullied mostly came back.

After years of delving into his life, I have come to admire, above all, the energy, the persistence, the defiance of fate, which saw Jabez at seventy-one trying to start a new life in

Burma, and which then, at seventy-two, took him on his final journey towards new employment in Wales.

But admiration fades when one remembers his victims. He took risks, which endangered himself and finally ruined him; but he also took risks which endangered others who had no idea that risk was involved – indeed, who believed that the names of good solid God-fearing men on the letterhead meant they had nothing to fear. He had suffered more than anyone from the crash, he claimed, but the evidence was all around him that this was not so. Emily Ekins, the maiden lady of seventy from Huntingdonshire, found by a coroner's inquest to have killed herself, her mind having become unhinged by the loss of the greater part of her fortune through the Liberator crash: she fared worse. Thomas Henry Pexton of Scarborough, who killed himself out of remorse at having persuaded his mother to entrust her money to Jabez: he fared worse, as did the widow and four young children he left behind. The schoolmistress, every penny of whose money was in the Liberator, who feared what the future held for her, and who most of all feared the work-house, perhaps ended her days there. And then poor Follinfant, dead in Greenwich Park, with his message to his widow and son in his pocket. There is much that one can excuse in this great Victorian rogue – but that is hard to forgive.

From Marble Arch, close to Jabez's grand address at Marlborough Gate, you can catch the number 98 London bus up the Edgware Road, past the end of Church Street, where Jabez went with his mother to hear the powerful sermons of

Jabez Burns; close to Cuthbert Street, where his brother Arthur terminated his life; and on up through raw cosmopolitan Kilburn until the bus turns left up Willesden Lane, past Chinese takeaways and Halal butchers and Afro-Caribbean restaurants and internet cafés, all scarcely imaginable in Jabez's day. Up the hill, on your left, just short of the Prince of Wales pub, are the decorative iron gates of Paddington Old Cemetery. When it opened in 1855 as one of the first of London's new municipal cemeteries, this was a lane through the fields. But even in 1878, when Clara Lucas Balfour, mother of Jabez, was buried here, modest terrace houses, of the kind which many families had been ambitious to buy with the help of the Liberator, were springing up around it. The Prince of Wales was built in 1899, replacing a wayside tavern; the council school across the road opened its doors at about the same time. By the time that Jabez was buried there in 1916 the town had the place surrounded. When in its earliest days the most intrusive sound in the cemetery would have been birdsong, today it is full of the hum of London.

Paddington Old Cemetery has none of the glamour of its near neighbour Kensal Green, where great men like Brunel are buried. Its most famous inhabitants now are probably Arthur Orton, the Tichborne claimant, and the architect Edward Barry, son of the more accomplished Sir Charles who built the new House of Commons. Jabez Burns is there too, commemorated by the first eye-catching monument you see on your left as you enter from Willesden Lane. It's surmounted by a bust of him, with an inscription that reads: 'This monumental bust of

Jabez Burns DD Ll D is erected in grateful memory of his remarkable energy and usefulness as a preacher, author, philanthropist and temperance reformer and as the beloved minister for upwards of forty years of Church Street Central Baptist Chapel, Edgware Road. He reasoned of righteousness, temperance and judgment to come – Acts xxiv 25.' A respectful distance away, in death as in life, is the last resting place of Clara Lucas Balfour: 'her children', says the inscription 'rise up and call her blessed, her husband also, and he praises her.' Beside her is her husband James, of whom the gravestone less demonstratively says: 'The fear of the Lord prolongeth days'. Neither lived to witness their son's disgrace.

To this gentle place, on 28 February 1916, there came a sad little party to witness the interment in the grave of his parents of the late J. Spencer Balfour: his son James and his wife, with their two young daughters Doris and Joan, and two other relatives. The gravestone bears no inscription to tell you that Jabez is there. The non-conformist minister who conducted the service preferred not to give his name to the *Croydon Advertiser*. A wreath and a cross composed of lilies and violets from his granddaughters, another wreath, with no name attached, and a bunch of narcissi 'with deepest sympathy from L. Scott' were placed on the coffin. Also a bunch of tulips, tied with a purple bow, 'from your lifelong friend E'.

Was this Ellen, the wife he had lost long ago to dementia, and now in the grip of an illness which would kill her seven months later? Unlikely. Perhaps it was Ethel Freeman?

Appendix: Balfour Group Directorships

The principal directors and the boards on which they sat

DIRECTORS	LBS	LAC	H&LIT	BSC	H&Co.	L&GB	REC
J. S. Balfour	68–86	67–85	75–92	84–92	88–92	82–92	
S. R. Pattison	82–92	67–92	75–92	84–92	85–92	82–92	
G. E. Brock	86–71 85–92	85–92	79–92	84–92*	85–92*	88–89	
G. Dibley	79–85 86–90	83–89	83–87	84–91	85–92	82–92	
Revd D. Burns	68–85	76–86				82–86	
L. B. Burns	86–91		86–90	86–91	86–90		
R. Booth	90–92				92		92
F. H. Rocke			90–92	90–92	92		92**
F. M. Coldwells			88–92	91–92			
Maj. J. Wright	86–92		83–92	84–92	85–92		
M. Theobald	68–87	78–92				82–87	
E. Barnard		89–92					92

*auditor   ** 82–92 auditor

KEY

LBS = Liberator Building Society

LAC = Lands Allotment Company

H&LIT = House and Lands Investment Trust

BSC = Building Securities Company

H&Co = J. W. Hobbs & Co. Ltd

L&GB = London and General Bank

REC = Real Estates Company

Source: Westminster Gazette Special

Bibliography

The main sources for this book have been:

Official records:
National Archives files FO 6-445 and -446; DPP 431

Books and articles:
Anderson, Sir Robert: *The Lighter Side of My Official Life*, London, 1918

Annual Register, *passim*

Balfour, Jabez Spencer: *My Prison Life*, London, 1907

Baddeley, Geoffrey E: *The Tramways of Croydon*, Broxbourne, 1983

Benson, E. F.: *As We Were: a Victorian Peep-show*, London, 1985

Cambridge History of Latin America, ed. Leslie Bethell, vol. 5, Cambridge, 1986

Cleary, Esmond J: entry on Balfour in *Dictionary of Business Biography*, London, 1984

The Building Society Movement, London, 1965

Cornish, C. J.: *The Isle of Wight*, London, 1895

Dilnot, George: *Scotland Yard*, London, 1926

Falk, Bernard: *He Laughed in Fleet Street*, London, 1937

Farquharson, Robert: *The House of Commons From Within*, London, 1912

Ferriday, Peter: 'The Jabez Balfour Story', *Architectural Review*, December 1968

Hammerton, Sir John: *Books and Myself*, London, 1944

Harris, Jose: *Private Lives, Public Spirit: A Social History of Britain 1870–1914*, Oxford, 1993

House of Commons Hansard 1880–85 and 1889–95

Kynaston, David: *The City of London*, vol. 2, 1890–1914, London, 1995

Llewellyn, Sheila, *The View from the Bridge: The Story of the Thames-side Villages of Clifton Hampden and Burcot in Oxfordshire*, Clifton Hampden, 2000

Longmate, Norman: *The Waterdrinkers, A History of Temperance*, London, 1968

Lucy, Henry W.: *Diary of the Home Rule Parliament*, London, 1896

Marjoribanks, Edward: *Famous Trials of Marshall Hall*, London, 1889

Morris, Jeremy: *Religion and Urban Change, 1840–1914*, Woodbridge, 1992

O'Connor, T. P.: *Memoirs of an Old Parliamentarian*, London, 1929

O'Hagan, Henry Osborne: *Leaves From My Life*, London, 1929

Priestley, Philip: *Victorian Prison Lives 1830–1914*, London, 1985

Robb, George: *White-collar Crime in Modern England: Financial Fraud and Business Morality 1845–1929*, Cambridge, 1992

Rock, David: *An Englishman in Salta*, Argentina, 1892–5 (in Burnley Library)

—'A Fraud Abroad', *History Today*, August 1999

—'Globalization in Cameo: a short history of a Victorian fugitive'

Searle, G. R.: *Corruption in British Politics 1895–1930*, Oxford, 1987

Spender, J. Arthur: *Life, Journalism and Politics*, New York, undated

Stead, W. T.: 'Two and Two Make Four (a novel based on J. S. Balfour', *Review of Reviews*, November 1893

Stenton, Michael and Stephen Lees: *Who's Who in Parliament*, Hassocks Sussex, 1978

Stutfield, H., 'The Higher Rascality' (March 1898) and 'The Company Scandal – A City View' (September 1898) in *The National Review*

Taylor, Derek and David Bush: *The Golden Age of British Hotels*, London, 1974

Vallance, Aylmer: *Very Private Enterprise*, London, 1955

Watts, J. Stockwell: *The Truth about The Liberator*, London, 1893

—*The Biggest Crime of the 19th Century,** London, 1893

Westminster Gazette Popular no. 5: 'The story of the Liberator crash, with some account of the life and character of Jabez Spencer Balfour'

* a third tract by Watts, *The Return of Jabez Balfour*, is missing from the British Library. Signed out to a man named Brown, it has not been seen since.

Newspapers and periodicals:
Abingdon Herald, Buenos Aires Herald, Burnley Express and Advertiser, Church Times, Croydon Advertiser, Croydon Chronicle, Croydon Review, Croydon Times, Daily Chronicle, Daily Mail, Daily News, Daily Telegraph, Doncaster Chronicle, Economist, Financial News, Financial Times, The Graphic, Illustrated London News, Isle of Wight Chronicle, Isle of Wight Observer, Isle of Wight Times, Manchester Guardian, New York Times, News of the World, Pall Mall Gazette, Penny Illustrated, Police Review, South London Press, South Wales Argus, Tamworth Herald, The Star, The Times, Weekly Dispatch, Westminster Gazette

Index